Acquired! *is a "must read" for all small business owners, whether they are for sale today, or are going to be in the future.*

> Brad Durham
> President & CEO, Independent Bank of Texas

John does a great job of giving you the scope and depth of selling your business. It is a clear blueprint in how to prepare to sell your business and get the best price!

> Ray Pekowski
> Chairman and CEO, The Expo Group

The principles explained in Acquired! *are not only "right on" but essential to the Business Owner trying to realize the greatest value for all their years of hard work. Where was this book 25 years ago when I first needed it?*

> Gary A. Dorland
> President (Retired), Security and Mission
> Assurance Company/ManTech International Corp.

You can flip this book open to any page and find something meaningful that you can use when you sell. This isn't 'theory'—it's full of practical tips and tools you can put to use before, during and after you sell your business.

> Ross Collard
> Founder, Collard Information Services

Wish I had read this amazing book when I sold my company! John Sr. has created a phenomenal masterpiece sharing how to navigate each of the nine stages of being Acquired! *This is one of those reads that's found a permanent home in my personal library!*

> John Deen
> Principal, emerging-minds

I loved reading Acquired!. *Was not sure if it would apply, since I am transitioning but could not put it down once I started reading. Very helpful information for preparing your company for any sale or transition.*

Charlene Sims
President, The Master's Press, Inc.

Unless you have an exit plan, you're going to lock the door and walk away with nothing. Acquired! *can help you realize something for all the blood, sweat and tears you put into your business.*

W. Barry Smith
Former SCORE business consultant,
U.S. Small Business Administration

John Sr. does a phenomenal job outlining a very practical, nine-step process that led to the successful sale of his small business. Take it from someone that has actually sold and exited his company well! Great and very easy read!

Stirling Vineyard
President & Co-Founder, CoVergence Group—
Succession & Exit Planning

Who better to teach you how to sell your small company than a small business owner who actually did it! Fascinating real life story!

Cynthia Brown
Owner, EA Tax and Financial Services

Are you're looking for practical solutions to sell your small company in less time? I mean, real life examples, not just a bunch of theory or complicated systems to follow? Then look no further!

Chris Wallace
President, Texas Association of Business

Acquired

Acquired!

HOW I SOLD MY SMALL COMPANY

Merged into a Large, Multi-national Firm

Barely **Survived** the Transition

&

Exited Debt-Free

John Arnott Sr.

ISBN-10: 0-9975762-6-X
ISBN-13: 978-0-9975762-6-9

DEDICATION

This book is dedicated to my family:

• To my wife Ellie, who has put up with my crazy business career for over 49 years, and still encourages me to keep going.

• To my son John—my business partner, clear thinking confidant, who always makes me look good through his efforts.

• To my daughter Michelle, my book publisher, loyal fan, who showed me how to dream, imagine, draft, write and publish this book.

• To my grandchildren - Austin, Lauren, Tyler and Grace—who will probably run and sell businesses much better than all of us.

Thank you. Yes, I am truly blessed by all of you!

Table of Contents

— ◆ —

— ✦ —

— ✦ —

— ✦ —

For Small Business Owners

I don't think I stopped smiling for a week after the direct-deposit check was in the bank. We had sold our company and in two days paid off our company bank loans, signed over the office lease, and squared up with our lawyers, accountants and M&A folks that helped us succeed.

Then, after 11 years of leveraging for the business, my wife and I paid off our mortgages, seconds and credit cards, and started taking the kids—and everyone else we could grab—out to dinner.

Wow, we really did sell it! And for the first time in our married life, we were completely **Debt Free!**

Actually it was two weeks of smiling. I know, because it was on Monday of the third week that the Integration Management Team of the buyer flew in, parked in our conference rooms, and started our four-month transition. Smiling was put on hold, at least for a while.

Is this book for you? It is if you own your business and

- *Thinking* of selling but not sure how to start
- *Want* to sell soon, and need a *Roadmap*
- *Tried* to sell it, and are now looking for a fresh new plan
- Have sold—yeah! But need to know how to *transition and/or when to exit*

If any of these apply to you, keep reading.

— ✦ —

Why this Book – Why Now?

I wrote this book for my four grandchildren: **Austin, Lauren, Tyler and Grace**. You see, ours is a family of small business owners, and it's a fair bet some of our four grandkids will be, too. For example:

• My son John and his wife Daisy have grown two technology startups and successfully sold both.
• My daughter Michelle started and now owns a successful book publishing business, built upon being a well-known author and international speaker.
• My son-in-law Chris is five years into a successful dental services business with his partner, and plans to sell in three years.
• My wife Ellen started and grew a successful nurse care business with seven nurses, and then helped one of the largest hotel chains roll out her concept in the U.S.
• And I have started and run 3 three consulting businesses, the second of which my partner and I sold to a large, multi-national firm. That sale process and transition is the subject of this book.

So, to help them, and to remind myself of what I will never do again—always do again—here's the book.

But the book is really written to help all of us
- all Small Business Owners

— ✦ —

After writing the first draft of the book, my daughter and soon-to-be-book publisher Michelle pointed out to me: "Very few owners have sold and even fewer been merged/transitioned. So, Dad, write the book for all of us owners out there now, so we do it better ourselves in a few years."

So I did. With you in mind, I have laid out a step-by-step process to sell the business in less than 18 months. It's a guide on how to prepare, time, market, and negotiate for the sale. So, let's answer your first question: **"Can we sell it?"**

— ✦ —

Part I:
Selling Your Baby

1. Can We Really Sell It?

- **Your Big # and Date**

- **The Sell Basics**

- **Is it Like Selling a House?**

- **Yes, Hire Pros to Sell It.**

—◆—

What's Your Big Number and Date?

My partner walked into my office one December morning. He closed the door slowly, signaling something was up.

"Ever thought of selling the company?" he asked, as he slid into the chair in front of me.

John, my son and 50/50 partner for nine years, was ready for something new. Before joining me, he had started and sold his own IT Database consulting practice to a larger firm. Luckily, for me, he then joined our startup, and we began to really grow. Things were going well.

"Yeah, I've thought about it," I said, "but I don't know how, or to whom, or how much we could get."

"OK, to start," John said, "simply tell me how much *you would need.* How much would it take for you to leave it all and be *comfortable?*"

I thought about it for 30 seconds, and blurted out a **really big $$$ number**, surprising myself when I said it out loud.

"OK, OK—that sounds good!" he said excitedly, "Now let's double it and add 25%."

He wrote down the number on a piece of paper and asked, "And when do we sell? How long to sell?"

I shot back: "12 months," and he wrote it down.

He then wrote out my **big number and date** on another sheet, dated it, and slid it across to me.

We sat there in silence for 10 seconds. Then we both started to smile.

Funny, as soon as that big $$$ number and date were on that piece of paper, *selling seemed doable.*

***

— ✦ —

So, before I continue the story, let me tell you who I am and what we sold.

I am a small business owner, a business strategy consultant, currently working on my third startup at this writing. I am old enough to have teenage grandchildren, yet young enough to still love being in business, especially the planning and growing stages.

I learned the consulting trade by being lucky enough to work at Booz, Allen and Hamilton in NYC, and later at PriceWaterhouseCoopers in Dallas. Those eight years grounded me in the consulting process and client strategies. Then, after a five-year stint at AT&T corporate—doing strategy work for their huge breakup—I started my first consulting firm.

In this first startup, I was essentially a one-man-band consultant, with just enough clients to pay the bills—most on time. I learned a lot of ways not to run a business, while waiting for the phone to ring.

Before startup #2, and needing work, I took a six-week engagement in Brussels, Belgium, for my former client GTE (now Verizon). The gig turned into three years, as I became the acting CIO for the Belgium Yellow Page Company, and later deputy CIO for the Belgium Telephone Company.

Returning to the states after Brussels—I and my new partner John II—hit success with startup #2—*Internet WaveTwo, LLC.*

WaveTwo grew into a successful 32-person IT consulting practice, fun to work at, and profitable. We targeted the healthcare industry, bringing business intelligence and managed services to hospitals and physicians at just the right time.

For 10 of the 11 years, I never dreamed of selling it until … John asked for my ***Big Number and Date***.

So, let's start with the sell basics.

— ✦ —

> *Now, I want you to know how you
> can sell your company too.
> Plus, I want you to know
> what <u>never</u> to do—what <u>always</u> to do
> before, during and after the sale.*

The Sell Basics

The week after we came up with our number and date, I came across an ad for a seminar about selling your business. It was a full day event in January 2012, put on by a national M&A firm. The M&A firm specializes in helping mid-market-sized business owners with mergers, acquisitions and strategic growth. By mid-market they mean companies with $2 to $25 million in annual revenue.

Basics in Just One Day

John and I found ourselves sitting with 25 other small business owners at the seminar. The event had an ambitious title: *"How and When to Exit your Business for the Most Profit - a Planned Exit Strategy."* It became obvious later we all had one thing in common—wondering *if* we could sell and *how* to price.

By the mid-morning break, we were getting into some meaty topics: realistic valuing, deal structures, finding buyers, packing proposals, and various negotiating techniques. Below is a summary of what was covered. But the Q&A sessions were as helpful and eye opening as the prepared material.

— ✦ —

Biggest Takeaways

A surprise for John and me was the **timing of the sale** discussion. We were told that almost 50% of buyers are looking for a company that is not only growing year after year, but is still on an *increasing* growth curve. Think hockey stick shape…

"Geez, who isn't?" I thought. But before I could raise my hand, an owner across the room shouted: "Hey, why would I want to sell if it's growing so fast? If I'm doing that good, I'll stay with it longer."

The instructor smiled and rebutted: "Of course you can stick with it until it starts to taper off. It will just take you longer to sell, as you are no longer in a rare place and hot market."

He went on: "But remember it takes about a year or so to get offers, even if you start today. If you wait until you start to plateau, you will find yourself in a bigger pool of sellers. Worse yet, if you waited, and your sales or profit estimates have dropped materially *during* due diligence, you could get a last minute reduced offer, or lose the deal all together."

It turns out his points were valid. More on this later.

Seminar Highlights

I recommend you attend one of these seminars in person. Online is okay, but we found the Q&A sessions and talking to other owners attending was as helpful as the prepared materials alone. Here are the highlights of what we learned.

1. **How to Value Your Business.** We learned just using simple price-to-earning (P/E) ratios, multiples and book values alone might mean you leave money on the table, or scare away potential buyers. The final price usually comes down to how much **value** your firm has **for the**

— ✦ —

buyer, in terms of a missing piece *or a strategic fit*. Topics covered were:

- Value myths exposed - P/E ratios, multiples and book values alone mean less money for you.
- Exit strategy and timing
- Demystifying M&A jargon - CAPM, discount rate, beta factor, terminal value, etc.

2. **How to Find Buyers and Package Your Proposal.** You quickly understand your business is more attractive to only a *select* **group** of buyers, and **not** *most* buyers. You need to think this through and let it be your focus, before you start writing your Offering Memorandum (universal listing sheet for businesses). In this session we discussed:

- Explaining your company's past; documenting its future potential
- Creating your "document of value"
- How to identify and approach the right buyers
- Which buyers to avoid and why
- Why your most likely buyer may not be the best buyer.

3. **How to Negotiate and Structure the Deal.** The takeaway here—you should *never* **negotiate directly**—have go-betweens until the meetings. This gives you greater flexibility, time to think, and new strength in asking for contract changes. We also learned about:

- Managing multiple buyers to obtain the highest possible selling price
- Deal structures designed to give you more cash with less risk
- How professionals may get the best price in the shortest time

4. **How Long to Sell Your Company.** We learned it takes about 12 to 18 months—on the average—to sell your company. They took us through

— ✦ —

a detailed 12-step process that requires at least 10 months before you could get an offer. (FYI: We had one real offer at 12 months, a second offer at 15 months and closed at 18 months.)

— ✦ —

"Is it like selling a house?"

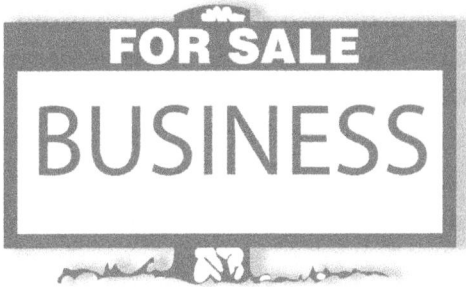

Near the end of the M&A seminar, the idea of comparing a company sale to a real estate sale popped into my mind. I dismissed it then as being too simplistic, but looking back now, it was pretty close.

To help you understand, I drafted the typical experience I have had in selling four houses (we moved a lot) and also selling some apartments we owned. Take a look, and see if this analogy is helpful.

— ✦ —

Sr's Analogy: House vs. Business

Selling Your House	Selling Your Business
Get your house in order • Remove clutter • Clean & repair • Add street appeal, etc.	Get your business in order • Update procedure manuals • Clean books for last 5-7 years • Remove unneeded overhead, and consistently underperforming staff.
Create an accurate listing sheet • Take pictures • Put listing on a national network • Send to your former clients, etc., and mail/email/text house overview	Create an Offering Memorandum (OM) • Squeaky-clean accurate financials • Put OM on M&A firms' contact lists nationally • Send a highlight sheet of the OM (not the full OM) to everyone above and update quarterly
Show house only to qualified buyers • Let agent show house only • Get offer and review	M&A firm handles all inquiries • Answers requests for information • Fields offers and communication • Acts as a liaison to remove emotional bias
Meet with potential buyers • Negotiate price • House inspections and title searches • Financial terms for payment	Meet with potential buyers • Negotiate price • Financial documents and due diligence requirements • Multiple meetings, written offer and financial terms
Close • Turn over keys • Receive payment • Transfer of ownership	Close • Agree to transition plan • Help management transition • Receive payment and turn over the business
Optional Hired Help • MSL Broker/Agent • Real Estate Attorney • CPA/Tax Accountant	Optional Hired Help • M&A firm • M&A Attorney • Tax Attorney • CPA firm/outside Accountant

— ✦ —

Yes, Hire Pros to Sell It!

Walking out of the session at 5 p.m., John and I went down to the hotel bar to talk. We had gone from "Should we sell?" at 8:30 a.m. to realizing at 5:15 p.m. "We need to sell *this year!*"

But we also knew we didn't have the connections or smarts to sell it ourselves. *But they did.* It also dawned on us we didn't have the **time to do it**, as we were *still* running a business.

So, we literally ran back up the hotel escalator and cornered the M&A director packing up the seminar material, and asked, **"So, how do we do this?"**

How It Works

The next week, we met the M&A guy at our place and took him through our firm, financials and what we had to offer. He honed in on our target market, growth strategy, and how we were unique. He thought we could sell for three reasons: our target market was strong, we had a good track record, and we were *still* growing.

Not quite sure of the process, we asked him to explain how he would sell us; how it works. He then took us through a 12-step process that included getting us ready, writing the Offering Memorandum (OM), marketing the OM, qualifying prospects, meeting prospects for us, setting phone-in and in-person meetings, and negotiating the deal. It appeared comprehensive, and they showed us their venture capital lists and sources of potential buyers. They seemed to have experience with small business, and a good success record of sales.

— ✦ —

We signed a contract that day with a $20K down payment.

We agreed to a variable compensation plan for them based on the final sale price. In turn, they agreed to actively market us for a minimum of two years, and to send out quarterly updates to all prospects. Also, with the incentive compensation plan, they could make more if we sold for more. And if it sold faster, it would also be more profitable for them. As it turned out, it was a good deal for all of us.

Who Else We Hired

In addition to hiring the M&A firm, we hired a **Tax Consultant** who ended up saving us a great deal of money. For example, we thought we had to sell the whole company, that is, all the stock. Not so. He showed us how we could just sell the assets—*and reduce our capital gains taxes by almost half.* Yes, by half!

To be on the safe side, we also used our own **CPA firm** to confirm the tax advice, and later to help us with updating the financials. The CPA firm knew us for years, and had all of our financials, but didn't know the M&A business. Oh, it turned out the tax consultant was right. ☺

We also hired an **outside accounting support** team to help crunch the numbers confidentially. We needed to keep it from our internal accountants and administration staff. **This was necessary to keep the sale process confidential** (more on this later).

Finally, we hired a **very good M&A attorney (hourly)** to read over the offers and give us advice. He also brought new **strength** to ask for a better deal. It's funny how some of the most mild-mannered, polite people have within them enormous **grit, gumption and nerv**e, to say NO and ask for more— time and again—and to do it politely. Lucky for us, our attorney was one of these rare individuals. ☺

— ✦ —

2. Listing the "House" You Built

Get Your

House
in
Order

• **Your Business's Listing Sheet**

• **High Quality Offering Memorandum – A Must**

• **Moment of Believing!**

— ✦ —

Your Business's Listing Sheet

In the M&A world, the **Offering Memorandum** is the gold-standard means to describe a company for sale. It combines an executive summary, with in-depth history and analysis of your company, and then <u>adds ground rules for prospective buyers</u> to follow.

It looks like the **Business Plan** we all talk about writing someday, but never seem to do. But instead of pie-in-the-sky sales and profit projections, it needs to be conservative and defendable to all. It has to answer the "why it will continue to grow" conversations coming your way.

I put the entire **Table of Contents** of the Offering Memorandum below. Note that every aspect of the business is covered in detail.

Where the M&A partner earns their money is in asking for more clarification and detail. *The best M&A partner **becomes the unknown buyer, probing** to better understand the offering.*

— ✦ —

Offering Memorandum
Table of Contents

Introduction
Confidentiality and Disclaimer
About (M&A Firm)
Inquiries and Next Steps
Executive Summary
Business Summary
Financial Highlights
Investment Considerations
Strategic Growth Opportunities
Products and Services
Overview
Revenue Mix
Consulting (what we were selling)
Pricing
Customers and Markets
Customer Markets
Key Customers
Geographic Markets
Sales and Marketing
Sales Strategy
Marketing and Business Development
Organization
Corporate Structure and Ownership
Staff Overview
Company History
Litigation
Facility and Equipment
Location
Facility
Industry Analysis
Industry Overview
Financial Analysis
Historical (Adjusted) Income Statements
Pro Forma Income Statements
Income Statement Analysis
Balance Sheets
Balance Sheet Analysis
Statement of Cash Flows
Acronyms

— ✦ —

Offering Memorandum – **Never Leaves the Conversation**

How you start is how you end. My mom repeated that phrase whenever I started a project. She knew if you plan it out and follow your plan, things somehow work out. Then she kept after me to deliver.

Fittingly Chris, our new M&A partner, took on that same mom-role as we began the Offering Memorandum (OM). He began by crafting a series of spreadsheets with lists of documents and templates we needed to complete.

He then designed a means to cross-reference our financials and pro-formas. We had literally hundreds of source material documents that needed to be cut down to about 40 pages. In additiion, we needed a system to ensure every number balanced, cross-fit and was correctly supporting other sections.

As helpful as the organization was to us, the M&A firm's analysis was more helpful.

Each document we created was sent through the M&A team and checked for reasonability. Especially in the beginning, they kept asking us to redo write-ups, and to prove— with more information—our assertions.

As the OM grew in content, the M&A firm provided a deeper analysis of what we were presenting, and suggestions on how to:

• Better present our strengths
• Proactively explain our weaknesses
• Discuss how we would fill gaps in our services
• And—most importantly—show how we would continue to grow.

To be honest, our initial tendency as we started the OM was to get it on paper so we could move on to prospecting. Wrong!

— ✦ —

> # What we learned
> - **Everyone is reading the OM for the details, not the highlights.**
> - **Interested buyers will use the OM as the literal basis for any contract terms.**
> - **Plus, the OM never leaves the conversation.**

The OM Never Leaves – Even After the Sale

For us, the Offering Memorandum never left the conversation. It became a constant artifact referenced time and again; before we sold, during due diligence, and after we sold. It became for us the most tangible thing about our company, before, during and after the sale. For example:

Before: Our prospect meetings consisted largely of us explaining our business first, and then responding to prospect's OM-related questions with more details. Unlike a house you could look at, the OM was the only tangible thing a buyer could review, so it was the jumping off spot.

During: Also during due diligence when the potential buyer gets to check out the contracts, sales, bank statements, etc. the OM was the item to verify. There can't be **any surprises** during due diligence if the sale is to close. The OM is the listing sheet that will either make or kill the deal, when financials and records are checked.

After: When we sold and were acquired, the OM became the literal basis for all of our sales forecasts for years one and two. Even if changes had occurred immediately prior to the sale, the OM was viewed as what was bought and what would be delivered.

— ✦ —

Hidden Benefits of Writing the OM

The OM provided benefits beyond the tangible business information for sellers. The process of creating the OM—and seeing the whole of our business in a new light—was a learning opportunity. We learned to rethink and change areas that were weak or just not existing into better strategies, tactics, systems, staff and management.

Each item we included in the document led to us changing parts of operations, finances, competitive stance, and growth plans. Why? Because of the questions the OM begged.

> **None of these were visible to my partner and me, until we finished our 4-month effort.**

Operational Issues:
- Integrated Offerings: Are they multifaceted, interrelated and synergistic?
- Employee Effectiveness: Is retention stable, efficient; is revenue per employee above industry levels?
- Visibility: Are we proactive in marketing and brand management? How?
- Management Transition: Do we want to stay? Will we need to stay? How long?

— ✦ —

Financial Issues:
- Operating Expenses: As a percentage of sales, are they decreasing? Why?
- Earnings: EBITDA % of sales over years – compared to industry leaders?
- Liquidity: Strength to satisfy short-term obligation; is our industry comparison favorable?

External Issues:
- Outstanding Growth Opportunities: How to leverage recent event and unique market trends.
- Lack of Competition: Why? For how long?
- Industry Outlook: Relied on nationally to know sources that support our forecasts.
- Strategic Growth Opportunities: Detailed specific new and extended services that directly support Pro forma growth estimates.
- Geographic Expansion: Our planned national rollout which would support our growth.

Increased Profitability
- In the 15 months it took us to find a buyer, we increased revenue and cut expenses; trimmed staff; hired better team; paid down debt; and opened a new line of business.
- In short, we FIXED ourselves to about a 5% profit in the first six months and closer to 12% before we were formally acquired in 18 months.

> **Even if you never sell, the very act of going through the Offering Memorandum process can materially improve your bottom line.**

— ✦ —

What to Expect While Writing the OM

Here are the highlights of **what we learned** about writing the OM:

1. **It's real work that** needs to be **done by the principals only,** with some outside help. For us, that meant the two of us, plus an outside accounting confidant we swore to secrecy, plus the M&A firm.

   It took us three months to get to a final OM draft we could all agree upon, and **four months to get it out the door.**

2. **You have to do it confidentially**, without any of the management team and staff finding out. We were advised that if the sale leaked out:
   • Key Staff may quit
   • Clients could start looking for replacements
   • Morale could drop
   …And these resulting in a big revenue drop.

3. **Financials have to be pristine; not just correct, but crystal clear.**

   For us, this turned out to be the best thing we did, as our new owners were multinational and *understanding* our financials was as critical to them as the numbers themselves.

   To make them pristine, we worked to present them in simple GAAP terms, with clear reasons footnoted for each revenue and expense shift, both historical and forecasted. We discussed in detail *the why* of our losses as well as the *why of our successes*, and what we planned to do to *not make the same mistakes*.

4. **It needs to make the case that you are STILL GROWING.** This point came up in every conversation we had with prospective buyers. Everyone wants a value, but also a company that is **on the upward growth curve**, and has not topped out. For us, we were on that curve,

— ✦ —

yet we had to reinforce why we felt we would stay on that part of the curve.

> **The Offering Memorandum (OM) is not just important. It *becomes* what you are selling.**

Moment of Believing!

For me, seeing the 42-page Offering Memorandum (OM) in print did it for me. Chris, our M&A partner, dropped it off once it was bound. Holding the hefty book, I thought, "This is really possible!"

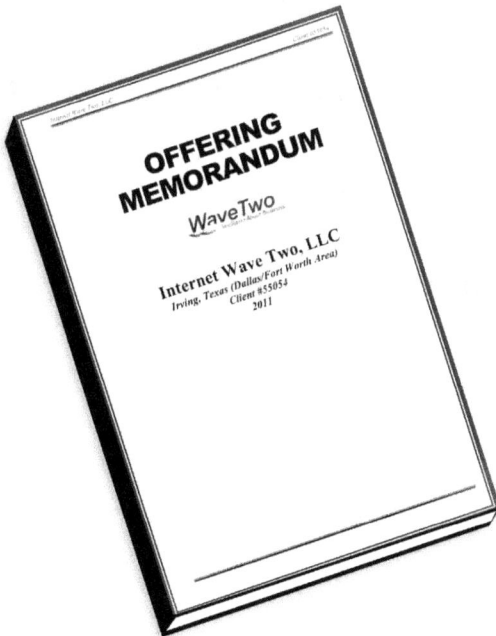

— ✦ —

3. Mail, Pitch & Fine Tune Offering

- **Mailing the Offering Memorandum**

- **Let the M&A Firm Do the Heavy Lifting**

- **Results of First Mailing**

- **Refine the Message**

— ✦ —

Mailing the Offering Memorandum

Send a Preliminary Listing Sheet First

Instead of mailing out the entire 42-page OM to prospects, we created a Preliminary Listing Sheet. Much like a flyer when selling your house, the M&A listing sheet is a one-page summary that keeps the seller confidential. Ours is shown below without the actual amounts and details, but you'll get the idea.

This approach is super because EVERYONE saves a great deal of time, and fewer non-disclosures have to be signed. All the important info is there, much like, "four bedrooms, three baths, with a water view" in a house ad.

If a potential buyer is interested, he/she contacts the M&A guy, asks for a full Offering Memorandum, and then signs the non-disclosure document before the full OM is released to the prospect.

After mailing out about 250 listing sheets (TWICE), we ended up getting about 35 requests for a full OM. Like house selling, it's a law of numbers.

— ✦ —

Actual Preliminary Listing Sheet

Here's our actual listing sheet – with contact and actual financials blacked out. By using a preliminary listing sheet, we were able to market ourselves anonymously until we received a signed confidential agreement.

Available for Acquisition

Niche Healthcare Technology Consulting Firm
Est. $▇▇m in 2011 EBITDA (▇%)

Business Summary: The Company is a multi-tiered technology consulting company that provides inter-related services including;

- **Healthcare IT Consulting** – High tech consulting services to physicians and hospitals converting from paper to electronic record keeping systems.
- **Business Intelligence** – Assisting clients in developing systems to turn raw data into usable information through the creation of platforms for data extraction, analysis, and reporting.
- **Enterprise Services** – Creation or improving enterprise level support of client resource planning and customer relationship management systems and platforms.
- **Managed IT** – Managing daily IT support including email, web, network, security, etc. for a fixed monthly fee.

Customer Market: The Company focuses on the healthcare market (63% of ▇▇ revenue) but services a wide range of other industries including finance (13%), manufacturing (10%), services (8%), and other (6%). Many of the Company's services are eligible for federal reimbursement and the Company has a number of contracts in place with government agencies providing a strong barrier to entry. As of December 31, ▇▇ no single client represented more than 13% of total revenue.

Organization: The Company is headquartered in Texas and has over 20 experienced employees. The owners have created a highly organized company with deep management (in addition to the two principals there are three non-owner managers) and a culture focused on sales. The owners desire to monetize their investment in the business for estate planning purposes and are willing to remain post sale.

Financial Highlights: For 2011, management forecasts ▇▇ million in sales and ▇▇ million in EBITDA ▇% of sales – consistent with 2010 EBITDA margin of ▇%).

—◆—

Let the M&A Firm Do the Heavy Lifting

Chris was our M&A partner who worked with us until we closed the deal. He came with a lot of experience in writing, presenting and closing deals. Better yet, he brought an attention to detail that we came to appreciate.

Phone and Physical Prospect Meetings. Our M&A group was very helpful in this area. Chris researched each of the prospects, and called them before we would take a phone conversation or meeting. Keeping us confidential, he would call each prospect, ask what they're looking for, how viable was their search, and if it was **budgeted.**

Our Screening Process. Then, for each vetted interested party, we followed the same process:
- Get a signed non-disclosure document from prospect.
- Mail full Offering Memorandum to prospect.
- Email/call with M&A partner about OM, and his insights on prospect.
- M&A would set up a phone call with us ONLY, after they confirmed the:

— ✦ —

○ Prospect was qualified to buy.

○ Prospect was buyer management or acquisition officer.

Results

- **250 OM Highlight Sheets Sent to Prospects.**
- **35 Non-disclosure signature requests obtained for a full OM document.**
- **10 Leads.**

Refine the Message

Our first step was to have Chris meet with every one of the 35 people who requested the Offering Memorandum. He represented us and determined if there was a true interest before getting us involved. Of the 35, we agreed to talk with 10 companies.

Chris then put together a list of key points for us to discuss with each company. This was helpful. Before we went on a conference call, we knew what they were looking for in terms of industry, market, customer base, revenue and timeline. It worked very well.

But We Lost Two Leads by Not Being Prepared

Of the 10, we blew two leads during the phone conversations because we weren't prepared. What we didn't have was a succinct summary of who we were, what we do, and a description of our target customers. We went through two painful phone conversations where the prospect would ask questions and we would stumble trying to answer them, talking over each other. Worse yet, these first two firms looked very promising, and had great profiles for growing our company. Ugh!

— ✦ —

Think Toastmaster Speeches

We finally got our act together. We created and practiced a series of small presentations on the most critical topics. We especially practiced responses to questions where John and I had slightly different approaches. To do so, we agreed on a standard answer to several gray areas, and then listened to each other during practice sessions to get them in sync.

This really helped in the in-person sessions later, where we were individually asked the same questions—when one of us was caught alone by the prospect. Our prospects just kept double checking us on their most critical questions.

We also wrote and practiced standard introductions to our strategies for growth, staffing, and customer service. When done, we had created about 10 presentations, which both of us could deliver, either on the phone or in person.

Don't shortchange this part. We blew a couple of good prospects because we didn't practice.

Fixing the Message and the Offering Memorandum

After the first meetings, we noticed a trend in the questions:

For example, we were asked each time *why we're successful* and *why we're going to continue to grow*. It turned out, the Offering Memorandum (OM) was too general or didn't address these issues. So we rewrote those sections and then took the opportunity to add more information throughout the OM.

Chris and his team then repackaged the entire Offering Memorandum, titled it an update, and sent out a notice to all the people they sent it to before.

The repackaging and sending out an update helped us, as it rekindled interest in some firms.

— ✦ —

If you go through meetings hearing the same types of questions, there may be something missing in your OM.

In-Person Sessions

After the update, we had four in-person sessions.

We were prepared this time, and we delivered good information and could answer all their questions. We gave ourselves A- and B+.

- Unfortunately for two of the four, what we offered was not what they were looking for to grow their segment.
- For the third—it was the money.
- And the fourth, well it was a maybe.

Not a lot different than selling a house we thought and stayed positive. We comforted ourselves by saying **ALL IT TAKES IS ONE GOOD ONE**.

— ✦ —

4. Your Baby is Ugly!

• **My Baby is Ugly?**

• **Counter-punching Ugly Baby Talk**

• **Not So Ugly Now!**

— ◆ —

My Baby is Ugly?

In sports, trash talk is all too common. It started with prizefighters at weigh in, verbally throwing punches, to gain excitement about the match and to get an upper hand on the challenger. And today, we even see it in professional football and basketball before big games. It's a way to get people up and excited, and also get your opponent to lose their composure and stumble.

"So what's this got to do with selling my business?" you ask. A lot.

Who Knew?

Do you think you would get mad, and possibly lose it, if someone trash talked your business? The business you built for years from scratch and for which you went in hock? Could you bite your tongue and stay cool and collected?

We didn't know it, but most corporate buyers and venture capitalists use this ploy to soften you up—to see if you can defend your business. They keep asking the obviously wrong questions to see if they hit a nerve. First, to see if you actually understand the business, and second, to test the assumptions implied in your business plans. They want to hear you talk under pressure.

Ugly Baby Talk—Sounds like…

What does trash talk sound like? It starts out innocent enough, even tame, and then builds until it starts to gnaw at you. For us it sounded like this:

"John Sr., it appears from your Offering Memorandum that your company is…

• Not scalable
• Too locally focused, yet said to be national
• Growing slower than industry averages

— ✦ —

- Planning on low margins
- Is in a red ocean
- Managed poorly and sparingly
- Selling to a concentrated customer base
- Based on a unique and crowded business model
- Possibly peaked and about to drop
- Under-capitalized
- Not funding new growth

...And is that your perception, John?"

"Not true! Not True!!" You want to blurt out after several of these jabs...but you can't. You have to prove they are mistaken and show them the light.

Counter-Punching Ugly Baby Talk

For this reason, we let the M&A partner handle ALL discussions with prospects, before a meeting. They could be objective and cool. We could jump off the track, and as such, blow a lead.

The prospect could dig, jab and be condescending to our partner, but our partner wouldn't get mad, just accurate and positive. We would then jump in afterward and expand on what was retorted.

Also, our M&A partner pulled questions out of the prospects. Their goal was to learn prospect concerns—the more the better. M&A members were looking for ALL the possible questions that an acquirer would ask, so we could explain accurately, and coolly.

After each preliminary session, the three of us (two owners and M&A) met on the phone, or for lunch, to discuss answers and rebuttals. In this way, we could then coolly and succinctly practice our responses aloud.

In fact, we did this about 10 times in preliminary meetings, as many of the questions were unique.

— ✦ —

We then held four in-person sessions and used the partner input to prepare.

In the end, the best thing is to have the M&A partner do most of this talking.

They know how to say—**Heck, This BABY is Gorgeous!!—and mean it.**

Not so Ugly Now!

Well after all those meetings and phone calls we finally got a Letter of Intent to Buy. Wow!

The first one was the biggest thrill, of course. We'd never had one before and now someone—who sat through qualifying phone calls, physical meetings with us and more follow-up phone calls with their management team—put together a letter saying they intended to buy us and here are the terms of the deal.

We felt great! Not sure if anything would happen, **but felt *somehow vindicated.***

— ✦ —

5. Learning the Letter of Intent Ropes

• What's a Letter of Intent – *really*?

• LOI #1: Doing it the Hard Way

• Dumb, Dumber or *Brilliant*?

— ◆ —

What's a Letter of Intent – *really*?

It's not a contract. Instead it's a **preliminary letter of terms**, describing the optimal contract offer, **if**—during due diligence—the following check out and are acceptable to the buyer:

- Financial history
- Assets and client contracts
- Leases and bank statements
- Revenue growth forecasts
- Staff knowledge and credentials
- Whatever

In our particular case, they laid out the terms as to how much the total purchase price would be, how much would be paid initially, and if there would be an earn-out provision. That is, how much revenue we would need to produce in a period to get the balance of the purchase price.

LOI #1: Doing it the Hard Way

Our first Letter of Intent (LOI) came **without a signature**. Yes, we later found out this is weird and not normal. Now to be fair, we liked this company. We spent a great deal of time with the acquisition team, and thought it a perfect fit. So, we continued, as we thought they were different.

They told us, to get the LOI signed, they needed the CEO—and his entire team—to meet us first.

After some haggling among ourselves and the M&A partner, we agreed to fly out to their offices along the coast and then spend a day with them, and so we did.

We got in the night before and met for dinner with our sponsors. The CFO for the company was our acquisition sponsor, along with the Vice President of Consulting. Theirs was a very large healthcare organization; and their Healthcare Consulting Services resembled our services. We had a lot in common.

Having dinner the night before was a good idea, as the CFO, our sponsor, pointed out to whom we had to sell, and to whom we had to focus on to close.

— ✦ —

And it turned out we had two targets to sell—the CEO and Chief Marketing Officer who worked largely in tandem running the company. So with that information, we felt very comfortable going into our session the next morning.

We had also received from the company a list of questions to be answered and to be expanded upon. We had prepared a summary handout and presentation—and were ready.

When the meeting finally began at 8 a.m., there were 14 people in the meeting room. Every C-Level executive was there, except the Chairman.

That was a good sign. These people were very serious and had brought everyone that would be involved with the merger. We then began by giving an overview of who we were and let the conversation go from there. We followed the outline they had sent, and we were prepared to answer and discuss over 200 points.

What were they really looking for? They wanted to know how we could integrate into their operations successfully. They liked us, but wanted our ideas on the best way to integrate our teams. We discussed it in general, and there were a lot of nodding heads.

The session went through lunch and we ended the meeting around 3 p.m. in the afternoon.

The Real Meeting—in the Hallway

At 3:05 p.m., we corralled the CFO and his VP of Consulting. "So how did it go?" we asked. He said: "It's good, it's really good."

"Where do we go from here?" The CFO came back and said: "I've already chatted with the CEO during the session and it's good with him. So now we're going to run it up to the Chairman, have him sign it and we probably should get this to you in about two weeks."

Well, we literally bounced out of that place. Driving to the airport, we

— ✦ —

were not quite high-fiving it but feeling really, really good. Chris, our M&A partner was happy too, but his boss, the **senior M&A partner** who joined us, **was positively glum.**

In the taxi he blurted out: **"What we have done was pretty much a cardinal violation!"** He continued: "All we have is a lot of good information and a lot of positive vibes but **no letter of intent** and, obviously, **no proposal contract.** And guess what? **We now have a new decision maker— the Chairman!"**

So he was **a** *little* **negative** about the meeting, but we were nonetheless very excited. In fact, so excited, we started working on the transition thing.

Dumb, Dumber, or *Brilliant*?

Yes, we created a transition plan after the meeting— without a letter of intent. Were we dumb, dumber or brilliant?

Working with the Healthcare Company's Vice President of Consulting, who reminded us that this was a done deal, we began working out the key steps to take us through the integration stuff. **We worked on it for about two weeks. It was a first-class business plan, and we sent it to them and waited.**

Then, about three weeks out, we got the news. The Chairman of the Board refused to sign the LOI, and he told the CEO and team to stop talking to us. Why? They didn't know. Was it our company size, our presentation, the integration plan? They didn't know.

We were crushed. **We were Dumber.**

— ✦ —

6. LOI #2: Better Outcomes through Bruises?

- **Nothing, Nothing, Then the Strangest Thing**

- **Ready for Them This Time.**

- **One Meeting, One Dinner, One Verbal LOI**

— ✦ —

Almost three months had gone by since our verbal-only letter of intent **bombed.** Frankly, after a while, we thought we'd never get another offer.

Our M&A group didn't give up however. They had updated our Offering Memorandum with our latest revenue financials, and sent it out again to over 250 more contacts of theirs. They also listed it—anonymously—on the M&A open market wires. Still, nothing happened.

Nothing, Nothing, then the Strangest Thing

But strange things happen. For example, instead of the new lead coming directly through our M&A firm, a small firm that had approached me three years earlier to sell, was purchased by a very large international firm. So one day I received a phone call from their acquisition guy (let's call him Bruno). He said: "John Sr., this is Bruno…and don't hang up! Are you still with your company and still doing what we talked about before?"

I said: "Yes and it's grown dramatically. We have around 32 employees and we're doing quite well." Bruno had talked to me a few years earlier and made a not-too-great run at buying our company. I was suspicious and a little cool to him on the phone.

Then Bruno happily said: "Well I am now responsible for acquiring companies for this large international company and I'd sure like to talk to you again about selling." Hmm—I perked up—and smiling, agreed to meet again on the phone a week later.

The next day, John, our M&A partner and I sat in a room, and we discussed if this was a good deal and what we should do next. We did research on Bruno, and he was right.

This was a very large international firm, and they had bought 10 companies in the last 12 months.

— ✦ —

The first thing we did was request that our M&A firm have a phone meeting with the international company and its principals. During the call, Chris confirmed that the firm had bought 10 companies in the last 12 months in order to grow their market share in the Managed IT service field.

They were interested in us, as approximately a third of our business was in that field, plus we had a vertical experience in healthcare—an area in which they had a very high interest.

So after a chat on the phone, our M&A partner picked up the ball and arranged a meeting of the principals.

A week later, the Division CEO of the company along with his boss, the SVP of International who represented all of its divisions in the United States, flew in from the coast. We met them in our conference room at the close of business, shortly after the staff left for the day.

Ready for them this time.

We had put together a formal presentation about our firm. But instead of giving a PowerPoint, we gave it as if it was adlibbed.

We had put together, especially John my partner, a whiteboard presentation that took them into sufficient detail about our business, our business model, and other key aspects. **We then proactively touched on every key question we had been asked over the last 15 months—but without the two of them asking a single thing.**

After 35-45 minutes of us standing up and talking, the senior VP representing the international operations said "That's similar to the approach we had put together."

Right then, John and I looked at each other and knew this was something very, very good. They had been attempting to do, with a large

— ✦ —

corporation, what we had done with our small firm. And in a city where they wanted a new physical presence: Dallas/Ft. Worth.

One Meeting, One Dinner, One Verbal LOI

Following our meeting at our offices, we went to dinner and talked for two hours. At the end, we got a verbal LOI. The SVP laid it out crisply, as he had done 10 times prior in the last 12 months.

"We would like to acquire you two and your assets. It would be for X times EBITDA, and require a one-year earn-out period. You would get XX% on signing and a balance when you meet revenue goals, as specified in your Offering Memorandum. But both of you have to come and stay a year. Are you interested?"

We looked at each other. "YES!"

LOI #2—Learning the Tax Implications of Stock vs. Asset Sale

We received the Letter of Intent from the SVP, with the provision that it be an asset sale. We didn't know what that meant. We thought we'd have to sell all of our company stock. Not so. An asset sale was just buying all of our assets (mostly client contracts and physical assets in our office and data center) for X number of dollars over X period of time. We were concerned that this could have terrible tax consequences, like paying 30+ % capital gains. That would kill the deal for us.

We talked to our M&A partner who recommended a tax specialist. The tax guy had just closed a consulting company like ours and knew asset sale law.

Asset Sale. The tax specialist did some further analysis and recommended proceeding. We had our CPA firm review his finding and they concurred. We qualified for lower taxes at capital gains rate, which in those years was at only 15%. **Happy days!**

— ✦ —

7. Due Diligence

expectations
evaluation
examination
exit strategies
investment
business
merger
fact check
DUE
DILIGENCE
performance
verification
risk responsiblities

- **Diving into Due Diligence Requests**

- **Meeting All of Management and its Teams**

- **Final Meeting Before Offer**

— ✦ —

Diving into Due Diligence Requests

Thrilled to get the LOI#2—Not so thrilled to get the following due diligence list

Five weeks and 150 hours of work later, we supplied, answered and re-answered the final questions and emails. We could now meet the entire management team for a two-day face-to-face review of this data.

— ✦ —

Title or Activity
Clients and Prospects
Complete "Customer Revenue and Services" Spreadsheet
All fully executed client contracts
All active leads/prospects in your sales pipeline
Financials
2009 and 2010 Financial Statements
2011 Financial Statements
2012 Financial Statements
Report of individual client profitability
Chart of Accounts and Trial Balance
Services
Overview of all services/offerings
Blank Templates of all Service Contracts
Complete "Services and Tools Matrix" template
Provide process documentation for remote and on-site service delivery
All states for which you collect and remit sales tax
Accounts Receivable
Client Invoices
AR Aging by customer as of the most recent month end
Client prepayments (deferred revenue) as of the most recent month end
Organization and Employees
Current organization chart
Complete "New Hire and Contractor Template"
Job Descriptions for all positions
Most recent performance review for all active employees
Engineer Utilization
Confidentiality, non-compete, and employment agreements for all active employees
Any agreements with independent contractors
List any employees that have H1B Work Visas, TN Visas, etc.
Benefits, Compensation and Policies
Copy of employee handbook and any additional company policies
Benefits prospectus
Vacation/Sick/PTO Policy

— ✦ —

Additional employee perks/benefits not listed above
Bonus and variable compensation plans
Payroll register
401K
Name of 401(k) Plan Administrator and Plan Record Keeper
401(k) Summary Plan Description (SPD) document
IRS 401(k) Plan Determination Letter
401(k) loan policy (if not detailed in SPD)
Outstanding 401(k) loans
Vendors and Partners
Complete all tabs of Vendors Template Sheet
Contracts for all vendors, partners, strategic alliances
All non-employee insurance policies
Loss runs for Workers Comp, General Liability, Property and Auto Policies
Company Vehicles
All real estate leases
Accounts Payable
AP check register
AP Aging
Credit Card Statements
Prepaid Expenses
IT and Fixed Assets
Complete "Fixed Asset Purchase Template"
Diagram of IT infrastructure (Visio)
Infrastructure summary
Colocation and Hosting Questionnaire
Legal Documents
Articles of Incorporation / LLC and Corporate By-Laws of Company
Current Business Licenses and Sales Tax Certificates
Tax Returns
Federal and state tax returns
Sales and Use tax returns
Personal credit reports of principals

— ✦ —

Meeting All of the Management Team
Two Days—18 Hours of Reviews—One dinner

The buyer team included 16 executives, by functional specialty, plus three levels of senior management up to the parent holding company. The review was extensive and well organized. Actually, we were very impressed with the level of detail and effort to get this right. To give you an idea of what to expect, here is the actual agenda.

Wednesday – Executive Strategy

Start	Stop	Topic
8:00 AM	9:00 AM	**Introductions/Review Objectives/Company Overview (both sides)**
9:00 AM	10:00 AM	**WaveTwo Overview of Healthcare Vertical** Critical Success Factors for Healthcare Vertical
10:00 AM	10:30 AM	**Break**
10:30 AM	11:30 AM	**Buyer Overview of Healthcare Vertical – Client Profile, Offerings**
11:30 AM	12:30 PM	**Lunch**
12:30 PM	1:30 PM	**Healthcare Education from WaveTwo (contd)**
1:30 PM	2:30 PM	**Marketing and Sales** - Marketing programs/tools, Lead generation, Sales process **Service Offerings – Break included**
2:30 PM	4:00 PM	What do you provide, how do you position on them: <u>W</u>ho does <u>W</u>hat, With <u>W</u>hat, With <u>W</u>hat tools and from <u>W</u>here? (5W's) What does your company offer that buyer does not?
4:00 PM	5:00 PM	**Tools & Process:** A discussion and review of all tools/equipment required to support the revenue being acquired. Infrastructure, hosting, licensing included. (5 W's)
5:45 PM	8:00 PM	**Exec Dinner – Principals**

Thursday – Tactical Due Diligence, Integration and APA

Start	Stop	Topic
8:30 AM	10:00 AM	**Client + Revenue Forecast** - Discuss top clients in detail, review health, client profitability - Review findings from contract review (assignment, terms, termination) - Validated/non-validated revenue - Revenue forecast for projects and on-call - Pipeline review
10:00 AM	10:15 AM	**Break**
10:15 AM	12:00 PM	**- Culture + Employee Review (HR)** - What makes this a great company to work for? Why do they stay? - In reviewing each employee, discuss (1) Fit, (2) Strengths & Weaknesses, (3) Role they play, (4) Skillset, (5) Importance to the revenue being acquired, (6) What role do they fit into at Buyer company?

— ✦ —

12:00 PM	1:00 PM	**Lunch**
1:00 PM	2:00 PM	**Benefits Review** - Comparison of Benefits - Where will we have issues? - Soft benefits
2:00 PM	3:00 PM	**Operating Expenses Review** - Review all expenses and vendors (what needs to be assumed vs transitioned) - Assumptions on length of transition expenses - Clarify any vendors/vendor contracts/pre-paid vendors
3:00 PM	3:15 PM	**Break**
3:15 PM	4:00 PM	**Integration Overview** – Kickoff Assumptions, pace of integration
4:00 PM	5:00 PM	**APA and EAs/Close Dates** – Review action items, exhibits, close timing

Game Day!

What happens in these meetings is what closes or loses the deal. It's Game Day.

Standing in front of the entire buyer management team, and then letting them question you and your partner for two days on every point in your OM (remember I said it never goes away ☺) was something else.

Before the Meeting

We had prepared for this meeting for three weeks. We put together a detailed PowerPoint presentation along with examples to address each of the 15 questions they had sent us. And then we practiced.

Going in, we felt that we were in pretty good shape and expected them to drill down on each one of the questions they sent in advance. We talked through possible questions and agreed on answers.

We flew out and met with the team at 8 a.m. in their conference room. It was made up of an impressive group of 16 individuals. In addition to SVP of U.S. Operations and the Division CEO we met in our offices, it also included two representatives from overseas whose approval would be needed to proceed. Also in the meeting were all of the CEO's Vice Presidents, the person responsible for our new Healthcare Vertical, the

— ✦ —

division CFO, Financial Analysis Teams, and the Integration Management Team. The only officer missing was the COO of the division.

Looking around the horseshoe of tables, I was impressed with whom they had summoned. A little nervous myself, I thought, they were taking us very seriously which could only be good.

Day One

After we went around the horseshoe introducing ourselves, the corporate SVP and Division CEO talked about why we were there and what they wanted to accomplish. They laid out for the group why they thought our company could fill a gap they were looking to fill. They asked us to give a brief overview of ourselves and why we were interested in being acquired.

I was the first one up and gave an overview—not only of the firm — but also my credentials. They were buying us too, so I discussed John's and my work accomplishments, and why we started our company.

I also spent a good 20 minutes scoping out for them the target market, the reason why our market was growing and why we had the services to successfully compete and grow.

Then there was a question and answer session. My partner John led the discussion on the 15+ areas that they questioned us on, and he essentially talked from 8 a.m. to noon. We took a brief working lunch break in the room, and ended at 5 p.m. We then went out to dinner with the international representatives and had a very nice dinner. However, even though you're having a nice time, it's all business: probing about ourselves, our backgrounds, and we were doing the same with them.

We liked them, as they were honest and smart. It was the end of a good day.

— ✦ —

Day Two

The second day started the same way. We began at 8 a.m. This session was designed to be the drill-down session. We had gone through the overview of everything. We'd described things more specifically to each of the 16 people, plus those on their phones calling in from different areas. These questions were to expose or at least detail what was right and wrong about acquiring us. And that pursuit went on for about six hours.

Questions You Never Expect

Near the end, we were all getting tired. We were also loosening up a bit as we were quickly getting to know each other.

Self-Assessments. They asked us to assess the quality of our organization. We were a professional service group and so in addition to our contracts, our most important assets were our people. "So tell us about each one," we were asked.

We reviewed 30 people and then at the end of it, the Division CEO said to me "So how would you evaluate John, your partner?" Then he said to John: "How would you evaluate John, Sr.?"

We looked at each other and then I had to give an overview of what John's strengths and weaknesses were in front of him. I told them how organized and smart he was, and that no one could manage a project any better than him. I also said, however, he sometimes had an edge that could put people off. Well, the reaction was amazing. Many of them piped up "Hey I got an edge too!" and so does XXX. Everyone could relate to John, and this one negative ended up being a plus!

And then, John had to do the same in front of me. To say the least, it was interesting.

After a few normal comments, he said: "And Sr. is the best at firing

— ✦ —

people. Even after being let go, they stop by my office and thank me for working for us."

"That's it? I can fire well?" I asked him on the plane home. ☺ I am still ribbing John about that comment.

Final Meeting Before Offer

Final Dinner

We were told at dinner that all 16 in the room recommended going forward with us. They added that a big reason was that they were impressed with our knowledge and not just our contracts. Or was it my ability to fire! ☺

Over dinner, they fleshed out the verbal offer in more detail. John would lead a national effort in Healthcare and be traveling a great deal throughout the U.S. to evangelize our services. He would not report to me, but to a Special VP of Healthcare, and other verticals.

I would become a Managing Director for Texas and surrounding states. My role would be to lead and guide the existing team—and transition the group into corporate structure.

We felt great. Of course, having learned about getting our hopes up during the last round, we were not ready to celebrate quite yet. However, we had all become comfortable with each other and continued the good vibe that had surrounded the meetings thus far.

Flying home the next day, John and I laid out our plans and discussed how we would structure our group to take it national. We were excited.

— ✦ —

8. The Written Offer

• Lawyers and Contract Revisions

• The (Reduced) Offer – What to Do?

— ✦ —

Lawyers and Contract Revisions

True to their word, a contract was sent to us a week later.

On the advice of our M&A partner, we had hired an attorney to review the contract. This turned out to be a very wise move on our part.

Our lawyer, call him Brad, was a very mild, pleasant man; low-key, but very knowledgeable of contract law. Plus, he was absolutely fearless in asking for changes to the contract. Working with him reminded me that it's always good business to hire people who know more than you do.

Our new attorney had worked with small to mid-sized firms like ours and had experience with consulting firms. He had worked with a number of our M&A's clients and so was well aware of what should normally be in these types of contracts.

Brad dealt directly with the Buyer's lawyer, spoke his language and asked point by point for more things and changes that we never would have thought to ask. For example, he questioned the domicile for where the contract would be located, warrantee limitations, and timing of payments, employment agreements, and more.

We went through the contract with him several times. And each time he was able to point us in a new direction. One of the things he said has stuck with me. I can almost still hear his words. He said:

> **"It's not what you sell it for—
> it's what you get to keep."**

— ✦ —

> **The takeaways for me were: Everything in the OM, our financials and transition documents has to be 100% accurate. You need an experienced contract lawyer for safety.**

Warranties and Accuracy

Warranties are a big part of these contracts. A warranty permits the buyer to get their money back if anything we presented to them was materially incorrect. That includes information in the OM, the latest financials, staff skills, active contracts, etc.

Fortunately for us, our lawyer was very good at the topic of warranties and was able to request modifications that gave us some leeway and more security. Also, to their credit, the acquiring company and its lawyer were very fair, too.

Not only will a good lawyer have your best interests at heart, but he/she will also make sure you understand what is expected of you in the contract.

Depending on your warranty obligations, it might be prudent to double-check that your obligations will be easily achieved.

The (Reduced) Offer–What to Do?

Well, we were feeling pretty good. The letter of intent turned into a draft contract, which we all agreed upon. We had verbal assurances the deal would close, and we were just waiting for a signed contract.

But part of the offer was dependent upon our latest financials matching or being close to our pro forma in our Offering Memorandum.

— ✦ —

> **After reading the email, I sat there quietly in my office thinking. This was _not the deal_ we were expecting or wanted.**

The last full month had dipped materially and our sales projections were now lower, too, from when we last talked.

I got an email from the Division CEO of the company saying: "John Sr., you may want to walk away from this deal. We can't make you the deal we quoted in the letter of intent. The numbers aren't there. But here's what we can do."

- The employment agreement would be for two years, and not one year.
- The earn-out would be after two years, not one.
- But you still have to hit your original sales projections for two years, even though they had dipped.

Also, the biggest change was the down payment and earn-out amounts changed. The down payment dropped and the earn-out went up— plus, no sliding scale of payments. Make the numbers, or no more money.

However, it was a fair offer <u>if we met our numbers.</u>

Also, we were very confident in our projections and numbers.

- We had a new <u>national marketing agreement</u> with a national physician products group that would put us in front of one-to-two thousand new sales opportunities.

- Also, we had just hired a <u>top national sales leader</u> at a premium, and two more statewide sales specialists, too. Between those new sales engines, and on top of our core business contracts, we could make, and maybe exceed, our numbers.

— ✦ —

• And finally, we had Monthly Recurring Revenue from long-term clients.

But, if we didn't meet our numbers, <u>exactly and on time</u>, even if they were just $1 short, their lawyer pointed out in writing, we'd get only the down payment. No sliding scale, just the down payment.

What to do?

I sent a text to my partner (who was on vacation abroad) saying: "It's not the deal we want. More risk for us; far less for them. More work on our part too. But, it's a bird in the hand. We could keep looking, but I say we take it."

And he came back and texted "Agreed. Done," and I immediately sent an email back to the CEO saying "Deal, done."

It took a week for the paperwork to be rewritten and when we received it, it was a large document with several sections. We sent it to our lawyer, CPA, support accountant, and M&A partner, who all poured over the sections. We had to turn it around in a week and July Fourth week had just started.

So there we were, my partner and I at a vacation summer home, on the front porch with our computers going through the document, all the while on the phone with the lawyer chatting back and forth, page-by-page.

> *Even then*, after reviewing the prior versions, we found things in the contract that needed changing. We sent our changes, some material, to their lawyer with our reasons. They agreed, sent a final draft back, and told us the date the deal would close.

— ✦ —

9. Is the Money there?

- **IT'S THERE!**

- **Paying All the Pipers**

- **So How Much Did It *Really* Cost to Sell?**

It's There!

When the deal closes and the e-documents are signed online by the principals, the money is transferred electronically to the seller's bank account. You don't sign a contract and wait for the check. You co-sign the contract online, and you look for the money in your account.

What's it like to see that in real time?

That day, I had been in contact with our bank. I told them what was coming, agreed on an account for deposit and sent the account details to the buyer's accountant. When I told the bank manager the amount, she got excited, too. "Wow," she said. I asked: "How will I know it's there?"

"Call me after you sign, and I'll look," she said.

John and I signed the contract. The Division CEO and Corporate SVP and CEO of the buyer co-signed the contract, and we all received the executed document in a secure email. It said, "Money deposited."

> **I immediately called my bank. When I gave her my name she yelled: "It's there. It's there! It's there!"**

What a rush! I still get tingly remembering.

Paying All the Pipers

A second thrill was paying everyone that we owed money. Within 24 hours of the money being deposited in our accounts, we paid all the outstanding bank loans and lines. The bank was not very happy to get the payment because they were going to be missing all the interest. But, hey, it felt great to us!

— ✦ —

> Weeks later, when we got our bank state-ments and clear titles back, we sat in our liv-ing room looking at them for a long time.
>
> We had never been in this good a position since we first married 45 years ago—so we just sat there and took it all in slowly one Saturday morning.
>
> Then we said to each <u>other</u>, "Let's go out to dinner tonight!"

We also paid all who made it happen: the M&A firm, tax consultant, lawyer, CPA and accounting support company.

Personally, the best feeling—for us, my wife and me— was paying off lines of credit that we ran up because of the business, and also paying off our home mortgages and our cars.

It just felt so good. The feeling of accomplishment after all those months of hard work, negotiations, and revisions had finally paid off.

It was a new era.

Assigning the Lease(s) to the New Owner

As much *fun* as paying off our debts felt, assigning our office lease was even more a *relief*.

You see, as a small businessman, unsecured loans and leases just don't happen. Not unless you own a public company, or very large private firm.

John and I were personally on the hook for the six-year leases. Our names were co-guarantors on the lease.

However, re-assigning the lease is no simple matter. Even with a large, multi-national company buying us, it still took the office leasing company five weeks to make the change. Our large buyer had to send all their finan-

— ✦ —

cials, and sign affidavits of their validity, and undergo background checks. Then, back fees had to be paid and contracts rewritten.

So, after 35 days of back and forth paperwork, we signed over the six-year lease to our new parent company.

This seemingly small act was like a symbol for handing over reigns to the new owners. Now the lease and the rest of the company were their responsibility. Sure, we still had obligations to complete, and work to be done. But removing the weight of the lease alone was a reminder that everything we had done up until this point had been worth it.

So How Much Did It Really Cost to Sell?

Paying Piper. Overall, it cost us about **9-10%** of the sale price to close. However, we had a pleasant surprise. Most of the fees were covered by a better deal price and an unexpected surprise on how to lower our taxes. Plus, we ended up paying 80% of fees AFTER the sale, with sales proceeds. Here's an overview.

M&A Firm – About 8% of Total Sale Price

If you recall the real estate house-selling commission process, and then add a down payment, you will get close to how M&A fees are calculated.

Down payment. To start, there is a non-refundable down payment of $15-25K, depending on your size. For this, our M&A firm worked with us to write the Offering Memorandum—a four-month task—and then marketed it and us anonymously through their national and international contacts. For the down payment alone, they agreed to market us for two full years, including prospect meetings and updates to the Offering Memorandum. **And they did just that for 18 months**, updating our Offering Memorandum three times and resending the updates to prospects and leads.

— ✦ —

Commissions. As they had skin in the game for up to two years, the M&A firm received most of their fees as commission at the close, based on the final sale price. If the company doesn't sell, they don't get the commissions.

For, us their commissions consisted of a minimum of $100K base up to the first $2MM of sale, and then a percentage for each additional million of the sales: 3% for next two million alone, 2% for next million, 1% for next X million, until you hit a cap. As the sale price rises, they get more but at a decreasing rate. Each M&A firm is different, but the idea is about the same for most M&A fees and commissions.

Hourly Assistance Costs: About 1.5 % of Sale Price Total

Our legal and tax support was crucial for increasing our net in-pocket return on the deal. We recommend this type of support, and find their fees a true value:

- Tax Accountant. A must, and not expensive. About 10 hours of support.
- M&A Attorney. Ditto—a must and great value. About 20 hours of support.
- Confidential Accounting Support. To keep things confidential from our internal staff, we used a known contractor controller to pull things together with us. About 60-80 hours.
- CPA Firm. These guys gave us another very much needed view at the financials. About 40 hours.

Part II:
Surviving the Merger and Transition

As we begin this part of the story, we are about as happy as any two partners can be, and we are eager for the next steps.

So how hard could this merger/transition really be? We had sold the assets, completed the paperwork, and we had a detailed transition plan to follow.

Well, it was really hard.

Much like having to step up your game, when you move from the minors into the majors in baseball, we found ourselves challenged at nearly every step of the merger and transition.

We got through it, and learned valuable lessons at each of the nine stages of being Acquired! These are lessons you need to keep in mind BEFORE you enter each stage. I summarized these lessons at the end of the book, and lay out the step-by-step journey for success.

Read it after you read this section—and when you decide to sell.

> **Frankly, I found writing this section of the book difficult: Difficult to acknowledge the mistakes I made and difficult re-living the angst and frustration.**
>
> **But feeling some pride too—in the hard decisions and unpleasant actions only a former small business owner could make.**

— ✦ —

10. Moving In

tran-si-tion 1 a: passage from one state, stage, or place to another: CHANGE b : a movement, development, or evolution from one form, stage, or style to another

- 150 Page Transition Roadmap

- Notifying Clients of Sale and Holding On

- People, Contracts, Titles and Money

— ◆ —

150 Page Transition Roadmap

We sold the company and now the real work began—transitioning into their business. We had heard from other people that the transitioning process either went really well or was something they wanted to forget.

We figured that it was going to go very well for us. After all, our acquiring company created a transition team with 20 people in it—had done it 10 times in the last 18 months—and had laid out a step-by-step process similar to our initial review process.

However, when we saw the transition roadmap, it had over 150 pages. It gave us pause, especially as we dug into the details regarding:

People	**Systems**	**Contracts**
Titles	**Billing**	**Receivables**
Money	**Collections**	**Reporting**
Processes	**Clients**	**HR**

Notifying Clients of Our Sale and Holding On

In the first two weeks of the transition, we had to notify all of our existing clients of our sale and integration into our new parent company. That alone was not a problem.

The problem was about 70% of our existing contracts did not have an "assignable to new buyer" provision in their contract. This meant 70% of our existing clients would have to sign a *new contract* with the new owner.

— ✦ —

Stressful Time

You have a finite number of clients and you're now giving 70% of them an option to rethink whether to stay with you. Ugh!

All of a sudden most of our clients *could opt out of their contracts*, unless we could assure them that the new buyer organization would be an improvement.

The good news was we weren't planning to go anywhere. Also, the services we had been rendering would not change and some would get better.

Relief and Compromise

About one-half of the 70% of our affected clients were okay with the change, if their currently assigned support staff—and John and I—stayed on.

However, the other half was not so happy. So, we ended up having to make concessions to these clients—in terms of pricing and service levels—to keep them. We didn't lose any clients, but we unsettled about a third of all of our formerly-smooth relationships.

> **Before you sell and sign the contract, make sure all of your existing client contracts have a provision that permits you to "Assign Contract to a future Buyer". If you don't, it could cost you clients, referrals and your business.**

— ✦ —

11. People, Contracts and Money

STOP
LOOK
LISTEN

• **Step 1: New Employment Contracts**

• **Step 2: Title Changes and New Pay Grades**

• **Step 3: Changing Management Incentive Compensation**

People, Contracts and Money

We held onto our clients with the changed contracts, but it was not as easy with our employees.

Step 1: New Employment Contracts

Let me give you some background. When our company was acquired, all of our assets (contracts and physical assets) transferred, but not our people. In the sales contract, our new parent had agreed to hire all of our employees, and at the same pay rate. An employee had to simply sign a new employee contract and all would stay the same. Sounded simple enough.

In our first full week together, each of our employees received a job offer and contract to sign within 30 days. However, a third of our employees (10) had problems with the contract, especially part-time work prohibitions and non-compete, post-employment sections. The non-competes were problematic for these 10, as the description of the type of companies they were not allowed to work for was by industry type, and very broad.

To their credit, the parent company's lawyer—a big help long-term—addressed each of the 10 employees individually, listened to their complaint, and then suggested changes to the contract they could both agree on.

In hindsight, it could have been easily prevented. The contract was never reviewed with us before presenting it to our team. We read it as they read it. Also, the non-compete sections were for those positions working only in a special area: Managed IT services. **Most of our staff did completely different work (e.g., business intelligence, big data, and healthcare systems), and the non-compete vertical areas shouldn't have applied to them.**

— ✦ —

Result of Step 1:

Of the ten who had problems with the contract, four of them eventually signed due to the changes. **However, six of them turned it down and terminated within the first month.** It wasn't the contract per se that pushed them out, we were told in their exit interviews. It was their perception that things would not be the same again.

Impact of Key Employee Losses

For us, the number wasn't just the issue—it was the loss of six critical employees. Those terminating were our COO, our head of Marketing, our most senior Business Intelligence developer and three other key healthcare consultants.

Worse yet, five of the six were billing time to ongoing revenue projects, which stopped when they left and didn't resume until they were replaced. To continue the projects, we had to scramble with temporary employees and reassignments. It was costly as the temporary employees put the projects in the red and pulled away key staff from other projects.

> **The transition started off poorly. We had 32 employees on day one and 20% fewer just 30 days later. On top of six that quit, we had another 10 that expressed concerns about the new company and HR issues.**

— ✦ —

> **Initially, our company (except me) reported to a National Director of Healthcare. She was able to get HR to agree to new titles and incentive compensation after several weeks. Then, after just 45 days together, she quit!…and the deal for titles with HR evaporated, and confusion began to creep into the void quickly.**

Step 2: Title Changes and New Pay Grades

We came to learn our company was **65% different from the parent company structure**. We were a consulting company, working on unique projects, each with different durations and outcomes. Theirs was a fixed price service offering with seven flavors. All their work was the same nationally. All their contracts ran three years, and their bills went out weekly. Period. Ours were more custom.

Also, we incented our directors and managers to sell new business and add-on work with commissions. However, the acquiring company had fixed pay for all employees' levels, except officer levels. We demanded our directors and managers bring in business, as well as doing the work. The new parent company would *not allow managers* and staff to sell, only defined sales people could sell.

So, coming up with a compromise started off well, but ended abruptly.

— ✦ —

Step 3: Changing Management Incentive Compensation

Getting the titles right *directly related to the salary grades and money.*
Once our directors became managers or supervisors, they could no longer
get any incentive compensation. HR would not allow it as it was different
from the other 500 managers and mupervisors in our division.

So, HR suggested they would give our management team raises equal
to what they normally were incented in the prior 12 months. The raises
would occur six months out at the beginning of the new calendar year.

Well, guess what. Come the new calendar year and the spreadsheet
with commissions for our directors, HR said they couldn't give them
those agreed-to amounts. They needed to be a higher level to get that
raise.

Now I was becoming another disgruntled employee.

Those first few months were stressful as our dedicated employees tried
to figure out how they would fit into the new parent company. Unfortunately, many were not willing to try to make it work.

— ✦ —

12. What We Gained: Better Billing and Collection Methods

PAST DUE NOTICE!

- **What the Buyer Did Well**

- **Professional Collections**

—✦—

What the Buyer Did Well

We found that our new parent had a great billing process and effective collection system.

They had fine-tuned their bad debt to keep it low, and their collections were high compared to other firms.

The company defined their service deliverables so that a client only had a small number of options. Pricing was fixed by option and by number of units. That is, the pricing for each of the options was based on the metrics of the organization: its devices, locations, hours of support, etc. So when a sales rep put together a proposal, there was no guesswork and no custom services. That was unlike ours, whose services varied by client and the quality of the person(s) assigned to the project work, and duration of the project.

While the parent's pricing and options may sound limiting on the front end, on the back end—for billing and collection purposes—they were ideal. These defined services permitted our parent to build software to manage every aspect of the client experience and help to scale its growth.

> **There were no surprises. All clients got the same type of services, and pricing was never subjective.**

While the billing process was an adjustment on our end, it was also a lesson in how to control costs and accounts receivable. We were starting to see the method to their business billing model.

— ✦ —

Professional Collections

Collections were another aspect of their business they did well. When a client became 15 days past due, the client manager got a note to call the client. If the client hit 30 days past due, the national collection group called the regional manager to complain. At 45 days, the national collections group took over and sent a letter to the client saying that they were in arrears, and their service could be discontinued within two weeks.

This approach worked for the most part. It worked because finding a new Managed IT Service partner could take months, and the transition even longer. So, the client generally paid. True, for some small clients, this was a time for them to leave.

However, the all or nothing approach had its downsides—that is, "if you don't pay in 60 days, we stop all services" could get ugly. Especially ugly for long-term and large clients who could not replace us quickly. It was also bad for the managing directors who wanted to hold onto client revenue.

Many times there were mitigating circumstances: that is, someone screwed up on our side and the clients refused to pay for a month. It does cut both ways.

We had a number of long-term clients who ran into some financial difficulties and we had given them time to pay when they got behind. One was a multi-million-dollar account with several hospitals we supported for eight years that got behind, and we had permitted payments to give them room to pay. However, as they hit 80-90 days behind, we lost control of the account to collections and upper management.

Overall, we learned a few things from our new parent on billings and collections, which we have already applied to Startup #3.

— ✦ —

13. What We Lost: Billable Time & Flexibility

- **Time and Money**

- **Downside of the New Processes**

- **Need to Push Back at CEO Level**

— ✦ —

Time and Money

While the people, titles and money issues were problematic and cost us staff, integrating into their existing processes and reporting systems turned out to be a huge time consumer.

As we started, we were told integration would be a one-month event. It turned out to be closer to four months.

In the first 60 days, we were spending 15-20% of people's billable time on what was supposed to be 5-10%.

Our business was more of a true consulting firm, project based with different variables from every project. Conversely, our acquiring company provided the same service with four or five different options all of which were clearly defined, price prescribed, and delineated in a single system.

But our way of managing projects could stay pretty much the same, we thought.

Transition Team

Our acquiring company had the foresight to put together a professional transition team as they were in the acquisition mode. As I mentioned before, we were number 11 of companies that they acquired in an 18-month period.

The transition team would come in, spend maybe two or three weeks onsite, transition all the employees into a specific position mold, train them on how to use the key parent software for the company (from initiating, monitoring, closing, billing, etc.) and then move on.

When I met with the Division CEO and his Senior Vice President during the sale process, there were assurances that the processes would be modified to adjust to our projects and project approach.

Overall, we would use the same approach that we had been using since our startup. There would be some modification for the way in which we

— ✦ —

managed projects and the way we priced them and the way we built them. However, that didn't happen.

The transition that was supposed to take 30 days ended up taking 120 days before we got to any semblance of normalcy.

The transition required that our entire management team be on conference calls Monday, Tuesday and Wednesday with various groups throughout the organization. It required our managers to spend an additional 10% to 15% of their time on reporting capabilities that we didn't have to do before.

We ended up having to change most of our processes and our procedures for tracking projects to comply with theirs.

If only we knew that at the beginning. We would have saved time, effort and held on to staff who left due to the confusion.

Downside of New Processes

The new processes started to wear people down. In addition to the six employees lost in month one, we lost an additional five employees.

These five employees were clear in their exit interviews. For example, we heard

• Our management team had shifted from decision makers to "explainers." They said "not sure who they really worked for now."

• Administrative duties had increased a lot, and they didn't like it.

• Company focus seemed to change from Healthcare services to mainly IT services of the new parent.

• Three employees told us they started looking in the first weeks and had quickly had offers from our competitors.

— ✦ —

> **We started with 32 people on day one.**
> **120 days later, we were down to 21.**
> **One third had quit.**

Need to Push Back at CEO Level

Looking back at the transition problems, they weren't entirely the new parent's fault. They were doing the same thing they had done 10 times before in one year. But they just didn't know how to manage a project based consultancy—just a fixed service offering.

It was my fault for not managing the buyer's transition team better. I should have not just pushed back harder on them, but instead, pushed senior management for relief and to get the exceptions promised.

We were told we would run our business with minor changes, but that did not occur.

— ✦ —

14. Owner to Employee

A New Reality

- • A New Place – With New Partners

- • Figure Out HR Fast

- • Make Things Happen!

— ✦ —

A New Place – With New Partners

As much as the transition and integration was difficult, moving from being an owner to middle manager was a new reality for me. True, I had some ego issues early on. But that passed quickly. It was having to learn how to **make my P&L numbers—as a middle manager only— that was unexpected.**

To manage profit & loss effectively, you need to manage all the parts, and react quickly. However, as a middle manager, simple things like hiring, firing, giving/withholding increases, and managing your clients are dumbed down or gone. What you now have is a new partner—HR—who makes people decisions, a regional support team that makes operations decisions and an engineering partner who makes client delivery decisions.

With this arrangement, you end up being more of a coach than a leader. And for clients, or customers, you learn to double-check with your operational/engineering partners before trying to resolve a problem.

> **In short, you learn to succeed by using a heck of lot of *implied* authority. You learn you are not in charge of "everything"— but still responsible to make your P&L numbers.**

— ✦ —

Figure Out HR Fast

The most challenging area for me after becoming a middle manager "Director," was working with a corporate/international HR group. They were high quality people, and professional, but we kept bumping heads on hiring and firing.

Why? I have thought about this a great deal since leaving, and I think I now better understand: HR's goals and my goals were far apart.

Employee Related Goals Not Aligned

• HR's Goals: Low employee turnover; No law suits; and No negative press
• Former Owner's Goals: Quality Delivery; Productivity; Increasing sales and high morale

The main thing in common was that both sets of goals included the employee.

Not Being Able to Hire, Fire and Give Raises

In a large corporation, it is common for HR/Finance to coordinate giving raises in order to be equitable and financially secure. Got that.

Also, hiring needs to be coordinated to ensure acquisition fees are under control and the on-boarding is orderly and legal. Got that.

But the Counseling/Firing method used by large HR I don't get—and you better get ready to solve this issue fast.

Frame of Reference: Before the acquisition, most employee performance related issues were resolved after counseling, and people stayed on in the company.

However, in some rare cases we had to terminate people, as they were not doing their job well, even with training and time to improve. Employees knew—from word of mouth and actions—that if they didn't improve, they could lose their job. Here was our process:

— ✦ —

An employee learned of issues through a supervisor's review (formal and informal).

- Performance problems were then documented, requirements agreed to and a warning given to employee to improve in 30 days.
- Most employees improved, and all was back to work and normal.
- However, if after 30 days there was little improvement, they were given another 30 days with a clear list of criteria of how to improve.
- If that didn't work, we terminated for performance or for cause and gave them two weeks pay. If it was a long-term employee, we would give four weeks pay.
- Most underperformers knew the firing was coming and had another job lined up within a month.

But at our new multinational parent company, HR made most of the counseling and firing decisions—not the VPs, directors, and for sure, not the managers.

Here's the process with international firms: If aafter a formal review, a problem is found:

- Each employee receives a minimum of three written letter warnings.
- Each letter is pre-approved by HR and must use a prescribed warning text.
- Each improvement cycle is four to six weeks long.
- After each cycle, the VP or director or manager writes up the results and sends to HR.
- HR is then on the call with the VP, director or manager, and the employee to review results.
- If termination is requested, a new request must be sent up the line.
- Termination is not permitted by anyone below the Division CEO Level.

— ✦ —

"So *what* you ask." Delays Hurt all Employees – Good and Bad

- An underperforming employee now has three to six months to improve. Not one to two months.
- Fewer underperforming employees are fired.
- Good employees see the lack of action, start to slow down and get discouraged.
- Worse yet, employees feel like they no longer have someone to protect them and decide to look for other jobs.

Make Things Happen!

Yes, I was frustrated. After 10 years of managing my own firm, I was on the sidelines coaching—trying to get more staff and not making my numbers to boot!

So, I decided to revert back to when I was working for large corporations—before I started my businesses.

Learning the game anew

I needed to relearn my middle management skills and to step up to making good things happen within a challenging situation.

So, I took our problems about HR up the line. I talked to HR directly and tried to work with them and get some exceptions to their timely processes.

— ✦ —

I used all of their internal recruiters to the best of our abilities in terms of getting them to concentrate on our needs. We talked to our assigned HR representative to try to get him to better understand how desperate it was for us to resolve these staffing issues.

We essentially went on the offensive, trying to work within the system and get something accomplished instead of just butting our heads against the wall complaining.

Here's what you need to do:

Learn how things "get done" in your new company.

Talk to owners who have been Acquired, and get their insights on who to work with and who to avoid.

Read the rules. If HR says you have 30 days, make it happen in 20.

Then PUSH! The ball will start rolling again.

— ✦ —

15. When Bad Things Happen—Plan for It

- Our "Bumps in the Night"

- Marketing Contract Voided

- Key Customer Contracts Abruptly End

- Parent-Company Support Pauses

— ◆ —

Our "Bumps in the Night"

We ran into problems no one expected or wanted. Now bad things happen to both good and bad people, so this section is not about us being unique. What follows is a heads-up for all small business sellers.

> **Things will go "bump in the night" after you sell, and it may hurt—a lot.**
> **You should plan for them,**
> **And**
> **PUSH a reluctant parent company to help you through it!**

Bump #1: National Marketing Contract Voided

Before we sold our company, we had worked one year with a national physician supply organization to market our healthcare IT services to thousands of physician practices, through their sales force which numbered in the 160,000 range.

> **We agreed and signed a two-year national contract, and was rolling it out as we sold the company. They planned to market our unique service through their large sales staff and existing client base of physician practices.**

— ✦ —

Our services were always designed to be national in scope and delivered locally. But for us to grow, we needed to find physician organizations that used our services—and not just in our local Dallas/Fort Worth area.

With the rollout underway, we learned we had to have the contract re-signed by our new parent company as the contract was not automatically assignable. We did the same with our clients, if you recall.

I sent the new contract to our healthcare national executive who was assigned to manage our entire business nationally.

In turn, she reviewed it with legal and came back within two days and said: "We will not re-sign this contract. They are charging too much, and it also goes against a number of other covenants that we have with our existing customers nationally."

I was stunned! Our business growth plan hinged on this existing agreement. I complained at the region and C-levels, but heard nothing back. I then went to the physician group to see if they would reduce the price and agree to other changes. They did.

> **The physician group agreed to modify the existing agreement to whatever our new parent company desired. I communicated their offer up the organization through the Chief Operating Officer and waited.**

To our surprise there was no response for three weeks. Then a brief note from the Division COO saying, "The contract will not be re-signed. Also, your company will no longer report to the national healthcare executive, as she quit."

Our entire team now reported to the Division COO, whom we never met before, was not part of our acquisition effort, and did not understand our business.

— ✦ —

Bump #2: Key Customer Contracts Abruptly End

About the same time, two major customer contracts ended with little warning.

Hospital System Goes Bankrupt

We had a large client, a healthcare chain of hospitals that were under our care for almost nine years. Our team did an excellent job for the client, and they were very pleased with our services. They were also a significant part of our revenue stream in that market.

They started to fall behind on their payments. Now, over the last nine years they were occasionally a month or two late, but they always caught up. Not this time.

Our parent's collection group got involved as well when they were 60, 90 and 120 days late.

Being a long-term client, we had our national collection group agree to give them more time, and we even had our senior regional officer visit with the hospital's CEO and the CFO to discuss how they could get back on track with payments.

Our client agreed that they owed the money and service was not an issue. However, they told us bluntly that they were trying to sell the entire hospital system and that they could not afford to pay us completely.

After getting some minor payments, payment stopped again. At that point, our national collection organization requested that we terminate the contract and stop providing any services.

That was the second bump, and it hurt! That one contract with all its hospitals represented about 12% of our recurring revenue. To make things worse, the past revenue that they owed had to be deducted from our historical revenue figures, making our P&L numbers look even worse.

— ✦ —

"Non-cancellable" Contracts Cancel

About the same time, another contract issue emerged.

We were a Texas state leader in helping physicians implement Elec-tron Medical Record systems. The U.S. government had given financial incentives to medical doctors to convert from manual processes and put in state-wide EMR programs to assist these doctors. One program was having a technology group help with the planning, implementation and certification of EMR use.

We had won three contracts with state agencies, and our work was well respected and documented. However, the first and largest of the state con-tracts was terminated unexpectedly after its program manager retired. His replacement felt they no longer needed us, and they would do much of the support themselves, even though we had one year left on our contract.

After written and face-to-face complaints to the agency, we considered legal regress as a last resort. However, our parent company—after analyz-ing the pros and cons—decided not to pursue action, and we pulled back.

These two lost contracts made for #2 Bump in the Night.

Bump #3: Parent Company Hits the Pause Button

We then scheduled a meeting with the buyer's senior management team to discuss alternatives to work our way back from these set-backs. Senior management included: two of the buyer's international sponsors for the USA, the international SVP, Division CEO, and Division COO, and key staff.

No two ways about it, we were on our heels and needed help. Our revenue plans were in tatters.

However, the only person that showed up was the Division COO. During that session, we reviewed with him the voided contract and ter-minated businesses and asked for help. However, he wanted to talk about

— ✦ —

why the contracts were cancelled and *how it could have happened without our knowledge.*

The meeting started tense and lasted several hours. Eventually, the COO came to understand that these things were a surprise, and we began to address how to regain the lost revenue. We recommended we restart the national sales contract with physician group. He said no.

We asked then to permit us to use the parent's national footprint, and sell via their 100+ offices in the US. He said no.

We kept pressing. We told the COO, in all the conversations with his senior management, the focus was on us being able to sell across the country. The national marketing contract would help us make our numbers, and if he couldn't give us permission to do that, he should help us sell our services through the parent company offices and regions in the USA.

> **He refused both requests. He told us not to contact anyone from outside of our local area (in or out of the company), and in fact, not to even travel outside the state of Texas. We were to just concentrate on selling in our local area only until sales resumed.**

At the end of the session, it became apparent that he didn't understand our business model. Worse yet, he said that if it had been up to him, we would never have been acquired.

It was a long weekend.

We were asked to pretty much pick ourselves up by our own bootstraps, rebuild our company from local-only clients, and to do it fast—in fact, right away.

— ✦ —

16. Reinventing in Real Time

- **OK, Now What?**

- **Popping for Recruiter Fees**

- **Re-thinking How to Sell Nationally**

- **Using Digital Marketing to Go National**

— ✦ —

OK, Now What?

We were stuck. Our desired model for national marketing and sales was halted, and we were now told to sell only locally—and not even regionally. Our healthcare solutions were for large prospects, and most were spread out in the U.S. But we still needed to find a way to reach out to this market—without traveling.

At the same time, our current salespeople seemed confused about what we were selling. Sales had been slow, but seemed to be worse when we told them to hold off on reaching out to non-Texas leads.

So we decided to do two things:

- **Find new**, high-quality sales people fast, with books of business to add revenue fast.
- **Rethink** how to market our services regionally/nationally. We were told we couldn't travel outside our Dallas market, but maybe there were other ways.

Popping for Recruiter Fees

Our first goal: find high-quality sales people to add revenue.

Our regional VP and his boss—the Division COO—were pushing for us to get new revenue and add new sales people. One had left and three were underperforming. They suggested I use the internal HQ recruiting agency, and I did for about four weeks. In that time, not one of the 20 resumes sent to me was qualified to permit even a phone call interview. Ours was a specific consulting sale in Healthcare and Development, and all the resumes they had sent were for Managed IT support sales.

I discussed the problem with my two bosses, and both agreed I could go outside to a search firm for help. I did, and I used a very well known search firm. In 10 days, we had interviewed three qualified candidates. Hooray!

— ✦ —

I had my two bosses do phone interviews with the three candidates, and we agreed to hire "Mr. Joe Superstar." We were all very up as the recruit appeared to have a book of business that could help revenue in the near-term. I made the job offer, notified the search firm, and scheduled a start date. The search firm sent their invoice (20% of the first year salary), and I approved and sent to accounting for payment.

Well, you probably guessed what happened next. Well, maybe not. Both my bosses got me on the phone and said that our multinational parent never uses search firms, and they never pay more than 5% for any job placement. And they had a national contract with the one that didn't work for us internally.

"Man! You have got to be kidding," I said. "Didn't we discuss this? And only 5%?" I was just stunned.

What I Did Next

I slept on it. Then I realized my direct management had no skin in this game, only my partner and me. If we didn't make our numbers, we would lose a huge bonus—our earn-out. So I told them I would pay for the difference. I would pay the 15% annual fee difference if they didn't.

They were surprised but quietly agreed. I called the search firm contact and told him the story. He was surprised too, but understood the gravity of the situation. I told him I needed this guy, and he agreed to take my percentage payment at the end of the year, and to bill my parent company the 5% now. He did, and we hired the guy that week.

P.S. The search firm called me back the next week and said if the super sales guy didn't deliver, they would drop my fees. Class Act!

— ✦ —

Re-thinking How to Sell

Our second goal: Re-thinking how to market our services regionally/ nationally.

Even with the new sales guy, we knew we needed to market regionally and nationally. Our planned national marketing got cancelled and we needed to reach out to prospects in a new way. We decided digital marketing via social media and email would be the answer.

Our old marketing model consisted of getting referrals from partners and former clients, and having our directors and sales staff call on the leads. It worked but took time and often required travel expenses—neither of which we had any longer.

My partner John had been following digital marketing and sales automation on various podcasts and websites. That is, using websites, social media and email to connect with prospects through online campaigns to gain new leads, referrals, and upsells, too.

One day, he and I spent a full eight hours watching and listening to new ideas from several digital marketers, and we began to learn. We liked what we saw and heard so much that we spent the next two weeks doing the same.

Here is what we learned.

Social media and online marketing can generate new leads by:

• Providing value to potential clients who reach out for more information.

• Accessing a broader audience, in a cost effective, timely manner.

• Building a presence and becoming known as an expert in the field.

• Targeting a specific client via websites, directories, and opt-in email.

It's almost like having an **"Invisible Salesperson"** on board.

— ✦ —

The Invisible Salesperson – Always Working for Us

Sales & Marketing Strategy for Growing Business

Attract

Target
Create an ideal customer profile and develop positioning statement.

Attract Interest
Attract leads through great website content, word of mouth and social media.

Collect Leads
Encourage leads to sign up to receive our content every few weeks

Sell

Educate
Create an experience that connects the buyers and guides them towards solutions.

Offer
Develop a sales process that aligns with your prospects buying process.

Close
Implement tactics that align with your sales cycle to close the sale

Impress

Deliver & Impress
Develop a great customer experience, and provide added value that delights customers.

Offer More
Develop a strategy to help generate additional and recurring revenue over time.

Source: Infusionsoft

— ✦ —

Using Digital Marketing to Go National

My regional VP was supportive of our digital marketing idea, but was worried about the cost. We estimated that it would cost about **$15,000-$20,000 to rebuild our website and begin the content generation, including a series of articles and videos, plus writing up targeted campaigns. My boss said to put together a proposal and talk to the Chief Marketing Officer.**

> **We put together a proposal where we (John and I) would <u>personally pay for the national marketing program.</u>**
>
> **Heck, we needed national leads and sales to meet our numbers, and if we didn't get new customers, we would lose a large earn-out amount.**

We reviewed the plan with the National VP of Marketing. He was somewhat cool to the idea, but appreciated our idea and funding offer.

We waited. We didn't get a "No" but no "Yes" either. Our offer was appreciated we heard, but needed the COO's and CEO's reviews and approval, too, to incorporate into the corporate marketing efforts.

So, we kept on creating our new digital marketing program while waiting.

— ✦ —

17. When & If You Should Leave

• **Keep an Eye on Your EXIT Score**

• **My Score**

• **When in Doubt, Look to Your Employees**

— ✦ —

Keep an Eye on Your Exit Score

Have Enough or Had Enough? A good friend of mine, a small business owner selling private aircrafts, often quoted that line above. I remembered that line in the first week into our transition, and then made a note to myself about what else it would take for me to leave this new, shiny business.

Here is what I wrote before we sold the company:

When to leave?

Do you still know the most?
Do they need your lead?
Is the original plan unchanged?
Are the numbers on target?
Are you still managing it?

Count the Yes's

4-5 = Stay
2-3 =Plan Exit Date
0-2 = Exit Soon

My Score

In 20/20 hindsight, I should have seen this coming earlier as my exit score had been dropping quickly over the last few months. The real decision to leave was determined by these five things shown below. Let's talk about them in order.

If you notice none of these talk about money.

— ✦ —

Do You Still Know the Most?

The parent company did things very differently than our project-based business. Although their knowledge was increasing, my partner and I still knew more about some critical aspects of the business. We had some unique clients and situations that could not be painted with the corporate brush, and we were the experts in how things were done. **YES**

Do They Need Your Lead?

I stayed there because my management team was looking to me for leadership. If I had left in the first month or so, they would have thought it was over, and would immediately have started looking for jobs. I held that off as long as I could. But now my managers knew the new processes. **NO**

Is the Original Plan Unchanged?

The original plan had changed materially. Our plan to market and sell outside of our local area was taken away from us—and as a result we could not leverage a large physician sales team nationally. We had also lost key management positions in the first month. **NO-It changed materially.**

Are the Numbers on Target?

The P&L numbers started to talk loudly. Well, you understand what that's all about. If the numbers are going up as planned, you can stay as long as you want. If they're starting to drop materially, it's time to plan a change. **NO**

Are You Still Managing It?

And finally, the fifth question asks if the E-myth goal had kicked-in. That is, has the team started managing without you? In my case, I was responsible for a region, a five-state territory, but my responsibility for staff had

— ✦ —

been taken away from me in pieces. My region had a person responsible for operations, a person responsible for sales, and a person responsible for engineering. The only people that reported directly to me were a number of administrative employees. The need for me was no longer there. **NO**

> **My YES score at 11.5 months was 1 out of 5.**
> **Time to Plan the Exit.**

When in Doubt, Look to Your Employees

For us, the company that acquired us—throughout the deal—was very fair and generous. Everyone involved in the negotiations, from International Corporate SVP, to the Division CEO, and all the way down to their lawyer, was fair and honest. For example, as we agreed to a two-year earn out, they guaranteed that even if we had been terminated during the two-year period, our salary would be paid the full two years. Very fair indeed.

We had a no-cut contract, and we could stay for as long as we wanted. Plus, the company paid us well, but...

I thought about leaving. I thought about it primarily from an employee standpoint. We had 14 employees left after about a year, down from 32. And I didn't want to let anyone else go. So staying might be necessary. However, the tipping point suddenly came one day.

During my weekly meeting with the Regional VP he concluded by telling me he would cut <u>all of our remaining staff</u>—if necessary—to keep his region profitable. So if we could not show a substantial increase and more sales, we would have to cut more people by month end.

What I decided to do was really simple. I spoke to my partner and said:

— ✦ —

"I'm going to recommend to them that we give up our two year no-cut contracts—if they agree to terminate our agreement in two weeks and they use that money to keep our remaining team.

The offer went up the chain of command, and they accepted my offer. The lawyers put the papers together, and we held a team meeting a week later to explain why we decided to leave.

Last Day

On the last day, we held an all-hands meeting in our conference room. The Regional VP was there and others from the region, too.

During the meeting, listening to the team's questions, and fielding old jokes, I started feeling better. I realized then that the small remaining team of 14 had gotten stronger, smarter, and were managing themselves.

While our sales numbers were dinged from bad luck— and some of my mismanagement—the 14 had nonetheless survived and grown in their new roles.

A year later, almost all of the 14 were still working.

— ✦ —

Part III:
Critical Lessons for
Owners at each Stage
of Acquired!

Stages of "Acquired!"

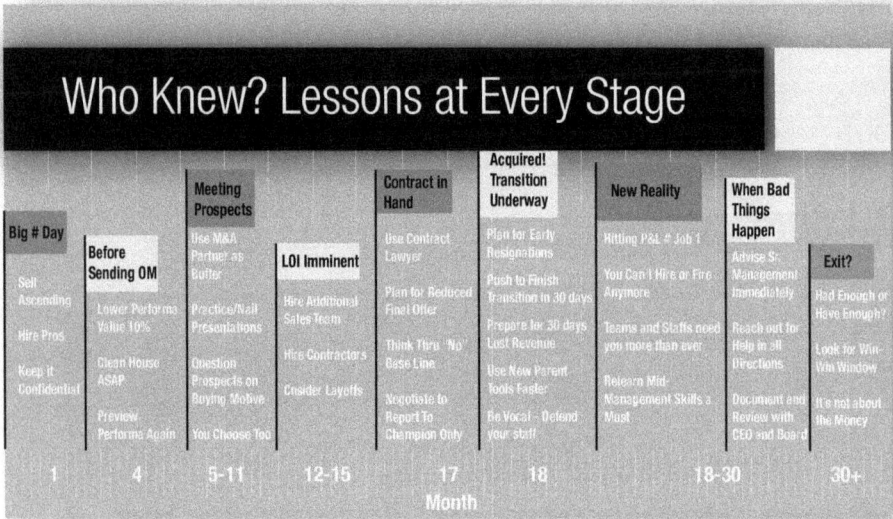

Who Knew? Lessons at Every Stage

Big # Day	Before Sending OM	Meeting Prospects	LOI Imminent	Contract in Hand	Acquired! Transition Underway	New Reality	When Bad Things Happen	Exit?
Self Ascending	Lower Performs Value 10%	Use M&A Partner as Buffer	Hire Additional Sales Team	Use Contract Lawyer	Plan for Early Resignations	Hitting P&L # Job 1	Advise Sr. Management Immediately	Had Enough or Have Enough?
Hire Pros	Clean House ASAP	Practice/Nail Presentations	Hire Contractors	Plan for Reduced Final Offer	Push to Finish Transition in 30 days	You Can't Hire or Fire Anymore	Reach out for Help in all Directions	Look for Win-Win Window
Keep it Confidential	Preview Performs Again	Question Prospects on Buying Motive	Consider Layoffs	Think Thru "No" Case Line	Prepare for 30 days Lost Revenue	Teams and Staffs need you more than ever	Document and Review with CEO and Board	It's not about the Money
		You Choose Too		Negotiate to Report To Champion Only	Use New Parent Tools Faster	Relearn Mid-Management Skills a Must		
					Be Vocal - Defend your staff			
1	4	5-11	12-15	17	18		18-30	30+

Month

1. Big # Day
2. Before Sending OM
3. Prospects
4. LOI Imminent
5. Contract in Hand

6. Acquired!
7. New Reality
8. Bad Things Happen
9. Timing Exit

— ✦ —

Now, I had heard that being sold, transitioned, and integrated was not all smiles and high fives. I had heard the horror stories from peers—especially after our sale was announced—and also from my new M&A buddies.

But, heck, this was us selling… And it was going to be different!

OK, it wasn't.

Critical Lessons for Owners at Every Stage

Take Action Before the Stage Starts

In the nine stages that follow, I outline the top lesson for each. And, I plan to use this list when I sell our next company in a few years.

So, for **my small business owner colleagues, my grandkids—and myself**—here is what to do before each stage of the sale process begins.

Let's start at the beginning. **Stage 1**— your **Big # Day**

— ✦ —

Stage 1:

BIG # DAY

As you figure out your big number and decide to sell, be sure you carefully consider when and how to sell your business. Here are three recommendations:

- **Sell Ascending**
- **Hire Pros**
- **Keep It Confidential**

Sell Ascending.

The fact is you don't get to choose this one. The best buyer will be scratching you off their list if you are not growing and have a steady track record.

If you wait until your sales crest, or are starting to decelerate, the buyer pool will shrink and also your company's value.

We would have loved to have sold during the 2009 recession, but we were not growing. After we recovered and started to accelerate in 2010-2011, we were able to make our move.

So, when you are in the midst of **some serious growth**, think about selling. It's usually the best time.

Hire Pros

You probably won't have the time or ability to market your own company. After working for four months with our M&A partner, we saw first-hand how much more they knew about the process than we did.

— ✦ —

Plus, using an M&A firm to build the Offering Memorandum increased our company's profitability. How and why? Our partner had worked about 25 business models like ours, seen best practices, and knew what our buyer niche was searching to buy.

Bouncing ideas off of them, we learned to rethink and begin to change areas that were weak or not existing. In the 15 months it took us to find a buyer, we increased revenue and cut expenses, trimmed staff, hired better operations team, paid down debt, and opened new lines.

In short, we FIXED ourselves to about a 5% profit in the first six months of the sales process and closer to 8% <u>before</u> we were acquired in month 18.

So, even if you never sell, the very act of putting yourself up for sale and going through the Offering Memorandum process can materially improve your bottom line.

Keep It Confidential

Keeping the sale of your business confidential—as long as possible—is highly recommended.

One key to selling your business successfully is to continue operating the business as if you were to own it forever. And you can't do that if there is uncertainty among your customers, suppliers, and employees. For example,

Customers: Your competition can use your impending sale against you. Customers, new and old, learning of possible new ownership may flee to a perceived safer, more stable competitor.

Suppliers and Contracts: If a sale is common knowledge, suppliers become hesitant to extend terms. It's the same for customers who become afraid to enter into new agreements.

— ◆ —

Employees. Knowing of a sale, employees—quite understandably—begin to worry about job security. They eventually focus their energies on finding a new job—rather than their current one.

With the sale known, circumstances can quickly derail your business growth before you gain any interest from potential buyers. Worse yet, your business value can drop before you meet the first prospective buyer.

Keep it confidential until after the sale.

— ✦ —

Stage 2:

BEFORE SENDING THE OFFERING MEMORANDUM (OM)

- **Lower Proforma Value 10%**
- **Clean House ASAP**
- **Review Pro forma –Again**

Lower Pro forma Value 10%

"The Offering Memorandum never leaves the Conversation," I said earlier, and it's true. And the heart of the OM—which the buyer watches monthly—is the financial prof orma statement. After all, this is a business, right?

And we all know, a good part of a pro forma is <u>estimating</u> which way the growth assumptions will play out. Calculating the numbers is an exercise in accounting combined with your best fortune telling, part art and part science.

For us, we were conservative and based our projections largely upon our existing contracts and sales pipeline. We factored down the pipeline too, but even then—in perfect 20/20 hindsight—we should have been even more conservative. Why? Because you want <u>to exceed expectations, not just meet them.</u>

But you may ask: "Won't that lower my potential sales price?" Yes, some, but that's not the issue.

— ✦ —

> **The issue is not what you sell your business for. It's how much you keep after you leave.**

So, when you have skinned-down your pro forma as much as possible, TAKE OFF ANOTHER 10%! You will thank me later, when you EXCEED expectations.

Clean House ASAP

As soon as you start to think about selling your business, get started cleaning house.

Taking stock of everything—from contracts, leads, operations and employees—will give you a fresh understanding. It will also give you a good start on gathering the remaining information you will need in the OM.

For us, cleaning house meant:

Counseling underperforming employees

Enlarging duties – promoting outstanding employees

Meeting with existing clients and evaluating long-term potential

Cleaning up "rosy" sales forecasts

Firing /not renewing a few clients

Reviewing outstanding project profitability

Restructuring a few projects

Physical reorganization of our facilities

New office signage

…and more

— ◆ —

Review Pro forma Again – After You Clean House

As with any draft work, one last review can be beneficial.

You've had some time since the first Pro forma. You now know more about your contracts and pipeline, and something probably impacted the Pro forma.

Things have changed.

Take a second look, and make it a bit more conservative.

— ✦ —

Stage 3:

MEETING PROSPECTS

- **Use M&A Partner as Buffer**
- **Practice/Nail Presentations**
- **Question Prospects on Buying Motive**

Use M&A Partner as Buffer

Potential buyers are precious, and you need to stay out of the way—until they are qualified and vetted.

Once the Offering Memorandum is marketed, your M&A partner will start making contacts to gauge the level of interest and to sell your investment opportunity to the market. The goal here is to get potential buyers bidding against one another and drive up the offers.

Let your new partner:

- Do all the initial contacts, and screen you
- Rebut all the YOUR BABY IS UGLY talk
- Follow up on calls and inquiries,
- And write up the replies.

Do this and concentrate on your presentations.

Practice/Nail Your Presentations

Winging it is for losers. Practice multiple versions of your business presentation and nail them so they are correct and precise.

Also, practice brings enhanced authority. You not only sound more authentic, you are now well prepared and—in turn—more effective.

— ✦ —

If possible, practice your presentation in the locations you will be giving it (i.e. conference room, office, hallways, etc.) and get feedback from the rest of your team.

Some presentations you should perfect include:

1. Elevator speech about your business
2. Why you started it. Why you named it X
3. The value proposition for the buyer
4. Your top markets and why they are growing
5. A much longer, full presentation (with PowerPoint or other visuals) that delves deep into the specifics of your business and markets
6. **And, answers to expected questions** that will come up during negotiations (your M&A partner should be able to help with this)

We found—the hard way—this approach worked. At first we were not prepared, and we lost leads because of a lack of preparation. We had the correct answers, but our stumbling hurt us and lost us Letters of Intent.

Take the time to prepare, practice and nail your presentations.

Question Prospects on Buying Motive

The truth is you don't want just any ol' buyer.

It is easy to cater only to the potential buyer and hope they are best for you. We did.

But you also need to qualify your buyer, too, by asking their motive in buying.

We were looking for a company that would take our local successes and help us replicate them nationally. We wanted a company that wanted us to scale and wanted our unique service to fill a gap in their company. So when we started asking, we found out quickly those who supported our goals.

— ✦ —

Our M&A partner knew what we were looking for, but it was still UP TO US to confirm their true motives.

Why is this important? **The buyer, and not you alone**, will need to deliver as promised, *after* the sale.

— ✦ —

Stage 4:
LETTERS OF INTENT (LOI) IMMINENT

- **Hire Additional Sales Team Members**
- **Line up Contractors**
- **Layoff Select Employees**

Hire Additional Sales Team Members

We didn't do this and got burned.

Burned in that we couldn't recruit quickly and effectively after the sale. Burned in that we did not have enough "feet-on-street" to prospect after we lost some key accounts.

"Sales fix everything," but only if you have the sales resources in place <u>before selling your business.</u>

So, hire additional sales team members. This will not only help alleviate the workload, it will ensure that a stable sales force is trained and working well before the acquisition.

Line Up Contractor Agreements

We lost employees unexpectedly after being acquired. And we lost revenue, as they were the ones that were billable. We ended up quickly hiring contractors to back-fill them, and it cost us in higher-than-normal fees and in some cases rework due to poor quality.

I recommend you line up **contractor support equal to about 20%** of your revenue producing staff. It sometimes takes a good amount of

— ◆ —

time to find the right contractors, so start as you await your first Letter of Intent.

Hopefully you won't need it, but line it up anyway.

Layoff Select, Borderline Employees

During the time you are looking for buyers, you need to look within your team and prepare a plan of action for borderline employees. These are people who are underperforming or unproductive.

You want to begin layoffs and terminations when you receive your first LOI. Also, if hiring additional staff, ensure all new staff are on board during the LOI period.

Why Now? Because if you wait until being acquired—and it's a big company—it could take months to terminate an underperformer (if ever) and months to rehire. Instead, do it ASAP, and you will be ahead of the HR curve.

— ✦ —

Stage 5:
CONTRACT IN HAND

- **Report to Your Acquisition Champion Only**
- **Plan for Reduced Final Offer**
- **Use a Contract Lawyer**

Report to Your Acquisition Champion Only

For us, the Acquisition Champion was both the Corporate SVP and the Division CEO. They knew us, our business, and saw how it could succeed. Sounds good, but...

> It turns out, **the single biggest mistake I made** was agreeing to have our company report to a senior company officer who was not part of the original offer, nor part of due diligence, nor the final offer, or even in on the several onsite management meetings prior to the offer.
>
> **We didn't know the person even existed until after the acquisition.**

As a result, this officer didn't know us as the Division CEO and SVP corporate knew us, nor even as the CFO and the entire transition team knew us.

— ✦ —

Because of that, he was not prepared to be our Champion and help us when we ran into problems.

When you begin to transition your business, it is in your best interest to report to the person you negotiated with during the sale. The champion is the person you likely made a connection with and the person you know is going to run your business when you are gone. This will save you unneeded grief.

Who and where you report to is critical to your success.

Make sure you report to your champion, and it's in the sales contract before you sign.

Plan for Reduced Final Offer

Ever had a garage sale? Of course you have, so you know that 95% of the time, you will get a reduced offer for one of your treasures—even if its brand new. Why? Because they can and you want to sell and they know you want to sell.

So, after three to four months of due diligence and multiple reviews of everything from people to contracts, what are the chances of a buyer finding something that might reduce the price? Well, it's probably not 95%, but it will be up there.

For us, our revenue numbers dipped during due diligence, so I should have expected a reduced price was coming.

However, I think we would have gotten a lower offer—even without the revenue drop—because of all the other variables reviewed during due diligence.

So when you get your letter of intent, think about how much less you might take—if need be—and where you would say no.

— ✦ —

> **Draw your *No Line* in your head and be ready with your bottom line number.**

Use a Contract Lawyer

A business purchase and sale is different from other sales contracts. It's more complex, plus it has elements that are extremely important for both seller and buyer—like warranties.

Warranties are a big part of these contracts. A warranty permits the buyer to get their money back if anything presented to them was materially incorrect. That includes information in the OM, the latest financials, staff skills, active contracts, etc.

Fortunately for us, our lawyer was very good at the topic of warranties and was able to modify and request modifications that gave us some leeway and more security. Also, to their credit, the acquiring company and its lawyer were very fair, too.

We went through the contract with our contract lawyer several times, and each time he was able to point us in a new direction.

One of the things he said stayed with me and I still remember hearing him clearly say:

> **"It's not what you sell it for—it's what you get to keep."**

Every dollar spent on a good contract lawyer is worth it. Make sure you find one, and take your time on the contract review.

— ✦ —

Stage 6:
ACQUIRED! TRANSITION UNDERWAY

- **Prepare for Early Resignations**

- **Push to Finish Transition in 30 days**
  - Budget for Lost Revenue

- **Use New Buyer's Systems and Tools Fast**

Prepare for Early Resignations

Timeline: immediately after the sale announcement

Employee retention is rarely 100% after an acquisition. Not every-one will be happy with the new situation and it is best to be prepared to replace people who may resign after hearing the news.

We lost six of our 32 employees in the first month, and five more in four months—for a total of one-third of our staff!

Fixes: Having contractors lined-up to fill in—especially on revenue producing work.

Also, hire additional sales staff before the contract closes.

If you wait until after you announce the sale, you may not have enough time to recover. HR will be a new partner, and staffing may be out of your hands once you close. Staff up before your announcement.

Push to Finish the Transition in 30 days—Budget for Lost Revenue

— ✦ —

Once the transition team is on-site, do everything to complete transition in 30 days. Take care of all processes, systems, billings, and client contact immediately. It is your goal to have operations in place—to be earning revenue—in the shortest timeframe possible. Setting up a transition plan will help, but unforeseen incidences will also creep up, so be prepared.

But even in 30 days, you will lose planned revenue. For us, we lost planned revenue in the first 120 days due to the transition.

Put the planned drop in revenue in your pro forma for months one through four.

Use New Buyer's Systems and Tools Fast

Time Line: switching to new processes and reporting systems from day one.

One of the ways to speed up the transition is to learn to use the new buyer's systems and tools. Lose the ego and move fast.

Remember, the buyer's systems will trump anything the acquired business is currently using. Loosen your grip on your systems, and move to the buyer's quickly.

The sooner all processes and reporting systems are in place and being used, the sooner the business will begin running successfully for the new owner. Although a drop in revenue can be expected, the swift adoption of new processes will lessen the severity and increase the speed of recovery.

— ✦ —

Stage 7:
NEW REALITY

- **Hitting P&L #s—Job 1**

- **Prep for Diminished Authority to Hire/Fire**

- **Be There for Your Employees—More than Ever**

Hitting P&L #s— Job 1

The reason the buyer wants you to stay is that they need you to hit your pro forma numbers. Also, if you have an earn-out, you need to hit those numbers to get paid.

> So in everything you do and plan have the P&L numbers in front of you. That is your job now. **Everything else the parent company can do for itself.**

Prep for Diminished Authority to Hire/Fire

During the transition, you will still be in a leadership position, but you may learn quickly you will have several people looking over your shoulder.

Most often you will not be able to hire or fire anyone without going

— ◆ —

through the proper channels and the parent company. Therefore, see that you clean house before you get a LOI.

Then hire additional sales and contractors before you close. After that, your staffing plans are up to the buyer's HR group.

Be There for Your Employees—More than Ever.

Your employees, especially the ones that have been with you for a long time, are going to be blindsided with the news of your sale.

Make sure you review any contracts that your employees may have to sign with the new parent, before you close. Look closely at the non-competes and dates of planned raises. We didn't and lost people because of it.

And don't underestimate the scary feeling your employees will all have at your sale announcement.

In a way, we business owners inevitably look like jerks because of the need for sale confidentiality. You cannot tell your staff you are planning to sell. So, when they inevitably find out about the sale, there will be a whole range of emotions.

Showing a strong, unwavering interest in their well-being will help the situation.

— ✦ —

Stage 8:
WHEN BAD THINGS HAPPEN

• **Document and Review with CEO and Board**

• **Be the Catalyst for Action**

Document and Review with CEO and Board

As an acquired company, a lot of careers and money are on the line because of you. Not only yours, and your earn out, but also the buyer champions that brought you in, the officers managing you, and all the way up to the chairman who asked the board to approve the deal.

So, if and when a disaster hits, send a complete account of what happened, why and its impact—fast. Think through what to do to fix it and estimate the new resources required. Only you can do this task well.

Events and time move fast, and word-of-mouth is sometimes misunderstood. Any and all issues need to be in writing and sent to the CEO, and copy your direct manager.

The buyer wants you to succeed, especially top management. However, if you report far below the CEO, he/she may not be able to help if not kept informed. Get it in writing and send details via express mail to all champions.

— ✦ —

Be the Catalyst for Action

Definitely reach out to the contacts you have with the parent company for help. Always utilize all of the services and options they have available.

Sometimes, however, you might find that the buyer's company, especially a large conglomerate, might be slow to respond. Don't hesitate to reach out for help in all directions.

If it takes money and time the buyer doesn't want to spend, consider putting in some of your own. A few thousand dollars could save you tens of thousands. To decide, balance what is at stake versus the cost and what will be lost if you wait exclusively on the buyer to act.

In any event, be the catalyst for action. It is your moment to lead.

— ✦ —

Stage 9:

AT EXIT

• Keep an Eye on your EXIT Score

• When in Doubt, Look to Your Employees

Keep an Eye on Your Exit Score—Monthly

The chart below helped me decide when to exit. Review it monthly after your acquisition, and give yourself one point for every "Yes".

- Do you still know the most?
- Do they need your lead?
- Is the original plan unchanged?
- Are the numbers on target?
- Are you still managing it?

Count the Yes's

4-5 = Stay
2-3 =Plan Exit Date
0-2 = Exit Soon

When in Doubt, Look to Your Employees

Of all the factors above, the one that impacts your staff is the most important.

They got you to the point where you could sell, and your leaving should somehow make things better for them—not worse. This needs to be the deciding measure—is it good for the employees, too?

— ✦ —

18. Next Step: Schedule Your Big # Day

I have been asked if I would do it again, that is, put my company up for sale and go through the whole Sale/Merger/Transition/Exit cycle again…with all the warts and drama.

ABSOLUTELY YES!

Why? Because selling is a very rare time in business life. It's that time when your peers—other small business owners—value what you have built and grown.

Of course, the greater value of our work is in improving the lives of our employees, partners and customers, and those lives are not to be minimized. Yes, for a very large part, that's why we are proud to be small business owners.

> **If the opportunity to sell presents itself, and you and the company are ready, and the deal is fair, go for it!**

It's the one time—maybe the only time—when we learn what the outside world really thinks of our handiwork.

— ✦ —

Thanks for reading, and good luck with your sale. I hope this book helps you speed your sale, smooth the transition, and keeps you smiling long after that direct-deposit check is safely in your bank account!

Sincerely,

John Sr.

PS: Please feel free to reach out to me with questions or to make suggestions at: jarnottsr@ContentFirst.Marketing

— ✦ —

19. Post Script: John Arnott Sr Today

So, what did we do afterwards?

Well, after a nice break of three months, John and I met and asked each other: "Do you want to do something again—together?" We both said yes.

We then spent six full weeks methodically reviewing 21 possible new business models. In the end, we found three businesses that were needed, solved huge needs, and ones we could enjoy. However, we had a hard time choosing,

Then one day, John asked me what would I do differently if we started WaveTwo over again? I thought about it and said:

> **"Focus and solve one area we *never mastered*: *marketing and sales*.**
>
> **We were great consultants and developers, and our customers loved our work. But, we never really learned how to market ourselves and sell consistently...**

— ◆ —

So, we created a marketing agency to help small business owners like us. We called it Clear Again Media, and branded it Content-First.Marketing

Our target market are small business owners who—like us—never really had the time to nurture prospects and leads, never consistently followed up on opportunities, and burned a great deal of money on sales staff who didn't close projects.

Different approach. We decided not to take well-worn "feet on street" sales approach using a group of salespeople. Instead we wanted a way to scale our new business with less staff, travel and overhead costs. So, today we market and sell ourselves—and our clients—using **digital marketing and online nurturing of prospects, leads, and existing clients.**

> **So, here's an even better reason for selling your business: you get to work and play at things that you have never mastered—and then reap an amazing new level of self confidence and success.**

So, let's do this…let's get Acquired!

John Sr.

John Arnott Sr., Co-Founder
Content First Marketing
jarnottsr@ContentFirst.Marketing
http://ContentFirst.Marketing

— ✦ —

www.ingramcontent.com/pod-product-compliance
Lightning Source LLC
Chambersburg PA
CBHW062005200326
41519CB00017B/4680